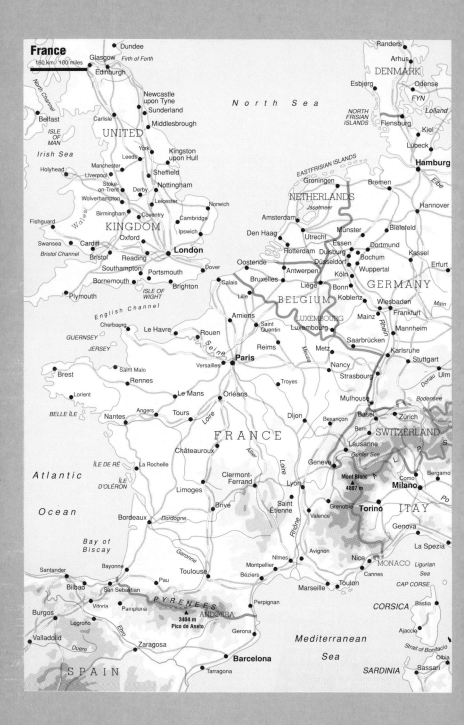

INSIGHT *pocket* GUIDES

alsace

Written and Presented by **Hans-Jürgen Truöl** and **Peter Schenk**

INSIGHT
pocket
GUIDES

Insight Pocket Guide:

ALSACE

Directed by
Hans Höfer

Managing Editor
Andrew Eames

Photography by
Hans-Jürgen Truöl and Joachim Ott

Design Concept by
V.Barl

Design by
Willi Friedrich

© 1994 APA Publications (HK) Ltd

All Rights Reserved

Printed in Singapore by
Höfer Press (Pte) Ltd
Fax: 65-8616438

Distributed in the United States by
Houghton Mifflin Company
222 Berkeley Street
Boston, Massachusetts 02116-3764
ISBN: 0-395-69013-7

Distributed in Canada by
Thomas Allen & Son
390 Steelcase Road East
Markham, Ontario L3R 1G2
ISBN: 0-395-69013-7

Distributed in the UK & Ireland by
GeoCenter International UK Ltd
The Viables Center, Harrow Way
Basingstoke, Hampshire RG22 4BJ
ISBN: 9-62421-521-9

Worldwide distribution enquiries:
Höfer Communications Pte Ltd
38 Joo Koon Road
Singapore 2262
ISBN: 9-62421-521-9

Salut!

Hans-Jürgen Truöl (top) and Peter Schenk

The majority of visitors get caught up in the Alsatian atmosphere a soon as the first scent of *choucroute garnie* tickles their nostrils; when they sip the local Riesling and admire the swathes of geranium that hang from half-timbered houses.

For us, the pull is both sensual and spiritual: after quaffing the second glass of Edelzwicker or eating a *baeckeoffe* in a *ferme-auberge* , it is clear why we return to Alsace time and again. The idyllic winemakers' villages – despite certain displays of tastelessness – don't look as if they are there just for visitors: the mountain world of the Vosges is wilder and more primeval than the Mittelgebirge on our side – that is the German side – of the Rhine.

Our selected routes in *Insight Pocket Guide. Alsace* are designed to show the contrasting facets of the Alsace region. After introducing you to the history and culture, we embark on a series of 14 tours – some city based, others drives through the Alsace countryside – which take in its loveliest villages, its outstanding natural features and with plenty of visits to the justly famous vineyards. Each itinerary includes tried and tested suggestions for eating out and accommodation; one tour (5), devised by our fellow writer Petra Klingbeil, is entirely devoted to Strasbourg's vibrant nightlife. Sections on food, shopping, festivals and the region's most famous products – wine and ceramics – supply background, while Practical Information contains essential tips.

In Alsace, they say, you learn to get hooked on comfort and pleasures. We hope this book will help. *Salut — Welcome!*

Contents

Preceding pages: Riquewihr,
a wine-lover's paradise

Following pages:
Traditionally Alsace

HISTORY

Les francaise de l'intérieur – the French of the interior – is how Alsatians often refer to their fellow nationals. They must suffer much more insulting references the other way around; a young Alsatian on vacation in southern France was called a *bosch* (a derogative French term for a German) because of his German-inflected French. Germany and France – formerly arch enemies and today, with the exception of a few minor crises, bosom friends – come together in the Alsace. And, when it comes to friction between the two nations, the Alsatians bear the brunt of it.

The history of Alsace is, more than anything else, one of eternal to and fro. It is the history of a patch of land which has been the stage for bloody conflicts; the history of a population which has been confronted over and over again with the nationalistic and patriotic ambitions of the respective victors – under whom they have amply suffered. In order to understand Alsace and its inhabitants even a little, you should be aware of the fact that, just between 1871 and today, the stretch of land between the Rhine and the Vosges has changed nationality four times. Someone born in, say, 1865 was forced

Fleckenstein castle ruins

le Culture

The prehistoric Heathen Wall (Mur Paien) on Mont Ste-Odile

into a patriotic high-wire act, during which the wire spun on its own axis several times.

The region's history is expressed most strongly and consistently through the language, as is made poignantly clear in an anecdote about an Alsatian whose name in French Alsace was Lagarde (guard or watchman). Monsieur Lagarde Germanised his name of necessity after the French defeat of 1870–1; henceforth he called himself Herr Wache (same meaning). In 1918, he became Monsieur Vache (cow) – the French pronunciation of his German name. Then, as the Nazis overran the Alsace in 1940, Vache was re-translated again; this time the family's name became Kuh (also cow). After liberation by the Allies the French pronunciation of this name must have been more than embarrassing – it sounds like a not-very-refined word for ones' rear quarters. The descendants of Monsieur Lagarde reconsidered the whole thing and decided it might just be better to retake the name of their forefathers.

Of course, the history of Alsace didn't first begin in 1648 with

La Petite Pierre

the Peace of Westphalia and slow incorporation into France, nor with the French defeat of 1871, but rather very much earlier. Long before then the Celts and the Alemannians had been there, the Romans left behind the tracks of their civilisation, and Irish monks founded an establishment which is thought to have had much influence. Bloody attempts at conquest occurred well before those of the Germans: the invasions of the Huns and the Hungarians and the horrors of the Thirty Years' War were certainly on a level with those of the two World Wars. Nonetheless, the Alsatians have indeed been influenced most strongly by being tossed back and forth between France and Germany.

In the 17th century the Parisian rulers had begun to subjugate the free imperial city of Strasbourg and the Alsace region, which was then splintered into a number of principalities. Mulhouse was able to preserve its independence because of its ties with Switzerland. The influence of the distant capital city stayed within limits – the Kings of France did not get involved in local affairs and limited themselves to a more-or-less representative display of power. This situation wasn't to change until the French Revolution. According to the doctrine of the Jacobins, the language of a free people had to be the same for all. Finally, if you truly had a French disposition in your heart, then you would have to lay aside your German garb as well.

The Alsatians never really embraced the centralism of the Jacobins, but the ideals of Revolution – liberty, equality and fraternity – certainly found many followers in Alsace. Thus Mulhouse finally joined the Republic. In 1989, when France celebrated – with a considerable amount of pomp and cash – the 200th anniversary of the French Revolution,

Alsace was among the real strongholds of the festivities – there was scarcely another region where so many productions and events were held. Napoleon also had many followers in Alsace.

The French language, however, has had a long hard road in Alsace. Simple folk continued to speak German or, more likely, the Alsatian dialect. French only gained a foothold among the bourgeoisie; it was the language of the educated classes. Perhaps Alsace wanted to be French at heart, but the language and culture remained German for a long time. For German historians and politicians this was sufficient basis for considering the Alsace a part of the German Empire. In contrast, the French interpretation of this matter flowed from the French Revolution – that membership in a nation did not depend on language, but rather on the free choice of the people. Not surprisingly, however, the Alsatians were never asked what they thought, and even when the scales were tipped towards France, there was never a referendum.

In 1871 Alsace was annexed by the German Reich after the defeat of the French in the Franco-Prussian War, and the imperial provinces of Alsace and Lorraine became directly subject to the

Eguisheim

Kaiser. A position resembling that of a federal state was not achieved until 1911 with the establishment of a state parliament. Starting in 1871 the Reich encouraged more than 200,000 Germans to migrate to Alsace, and a number of the French-oriented bourgeoisie left the region. With the new customs borders established in the Vosges, Alsace lost the economic hinterlands that it had previously controlled. German rule, up to 1918, also had its positive sides: Alsace profited from the modernising thrust of Wilhelminian industrialisation, urban planning and social policies.

This notwithstanding, after World War I, the people of Alsace were delighted to belong to France again. The French president regarded the jubilation as tantamount to a referendum. In fact, France was able to build on an immense burst of confidence. It managed, though, to mess things up in a very short time with a number of incompetent and bungling measures. France wanted to bind Alsace – which had been estranged through 50 years of German rule – strongly into the French Republic again. A selection commission was formed which classified members of the population according to the degree of their German or French ancestry. French was introduced as the official language even though only 10 per cent of the population had mastered it. An attempt was made to adjust the laws of Alsace to harmonise with those of France. It remained, however, only an attempt: Alsatians took to the barricades. They did not want their progressive social legislation taken from them, and the introduction of the separation of Church and State and a strengthened role for lay-people led to school strikes and demonstrations. The centralism of Paris broke its teeth on the thick – and determined – skulls of the Alsatians. It wouldn't be the last time. The assimilation attempt ran aground; even today the local laws of the Alsatians still contain numerous special provisions – and woe to anyone who tries to touch them. Thus, in the Alsace, there are still Church-run grammar schools, and the highest church official in Strasbourg is – at least in theory – appointed by the Republican head of state, François Mitterand.

These unfortunate efforts at assimilation did have one result: they helped Alsatian regional and autonomous movements – which came into existence during the Kaiser phase – gain popular support for the first time. These stood up for stronger self-administration and demanded from Paris that it respect the important positions of religion and the Alsatian dialect. Prohibitions, arrests and legal proceedings only led to the explosive success of the regional movement at the polls: in 1928, 11 out of 16 members of the local parliament were affiliated to the regional movement. Small splinter-groups, how-

Murbach Monastery

ever, drifted to the extreme right and worked with the Nazis in their *de facto* annexation of the province. As a result, for decades afterwards, any regional movement in the Alsace was discredited.

During the four-year period of Nazi occupation the Germans proceeded – with their characteristic thoroughness – to funnel the Prussian essence into the Alsatians and try to stamp out their romantic spirit. The wearing of berets was forbidden, the speaking of French in public punished, and family and christian names were Germanised. Prussian order and discipline came to roost. The Rue du Sauvage in Mulhouse – the 'Street of Savages' – was quickly renamed Adolf-Hitler-Straße (an ironic coincidence?). In the following year a number of Alsatians were either deported, ending up in the Schirmeck 'security' camp or the Struthof concentration camp, or were drafted into forced labour.

Some 140,000 men from Alsace and Lorraine were forcibly conscripted into the German army. To keep them from deserting, the *malgré nous* – as they were called in Alsace – were mostly sent off to the Russian Front. Those who were not killed ended up in Soviet camps where they often died in the miserable conditions. Around 50,000 forced draftees may have have died in World War II and afterwards. Compensation from the German government dragged out into the 1980s, and, even for the French, the *malgré nous* were, for a long time, a rather uncomfortable living momument – reminding them of the fact that France submitted to the 1940 annexation of Alsace-Lorraine without objection. After the war no Alsatians ventured a

Memorial on the Maginot-Line near Marckolsheim

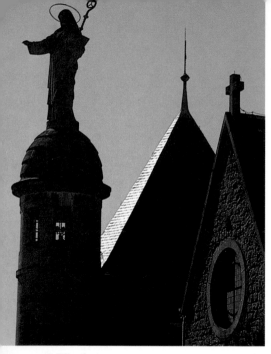

Odilienberg

protest against assimilation. What Paris had not been able to achieve through intense pressure, Hitler had taken care of. In order to fend off any suspicion of being pro-German, people presented themselves as 150 per cent nationalist: how else is it to be explained that many of the villages which, before the war, were solid supporters of the autonomists and regionalists yielded record results for the Gaullists? *Il est chic de parler francais* – so went the election motto. It was not until the train of events connected with the uprisings in 1968 that regionalism was newly discovered and the regional culture again went on the offensive toward the outer world. Even so, declining use of the dialect still could not be stopped. Today just 65 per cent of the population still speak Alsatian and the number is declining, especially in the cities. Inevitably, the number of Alsatians who speak German is also on the way down. Thus in the last 10 years the circulation of the bilingual editions of both Alsatian regional newspapers has diminished considerably. Quite recently, however, the importance of linguistic versatility seems to have been recognised. German instruction is mandatory in the schools and the Alsatian regional politicians are heavily in favour of bilingualism. The reunification of Germany supports this development. And if one wishes to have an economic voice in Eastern Europe, knowledge of German is indispensable. In Alsace it is felt that the region is practically predestined to be France's gateway to the East. For centuries the Alsatians have suffered the rampages of history; today it appears as though their position between Germany and France might just turn out to be for the best.

Culture

Besides its culinary excellence and the beauty of its landscape, Alsace also attracts visitors with its abundance of cultural monuments, the great number of interesting and significant churches, its historic city centres, museums and works of art.

The Romans left their mark in the excellent construction and extension of trading roads and, not least, through the introduction of that herbaceous vine whose precious juice sends many visitors into fits of rapture: the wine grape. A number of Alsatian museums house excavation finds from the Roman period.

The art treasures of Alsace have been considerably influenced by Christianity, which first appeared toward the end of the fourth century and celebrated its triumphal procession in the seventh century. One testimonial to this is the famous monastery church of Murbach — for centuries the abbey maintained a considerable influence in southern Alsace. The presence of the Alemannians means that the region still has a close linguistic and cultural kinship with their neighbours in northern Switzerland and in the German region of Baden.

Architecture in the Alsace began with the works of the Carolingians. Their churches have all been replaced, though, especially during the Romanesque period. As evidence of late Carolingian architecture an octagonal church has survived in Ottmarsheim, built in the year 1050 and a smaller version of the parish chapel in Aachen, Germany.

Phalsbourg, man of iron

The rule of the Hohenstauffen dynasty, in the 12th and 13th centuries, is considered to have been a golden age for Alsace — a period during which many cities were founded as well as churches and castles built. From 1268, with the passing of the Hohenstauffen period, the slow conversion began from Romanesque to Gothic building styles. Thus, Strasbourg Cathedral — originally planned to be Romanesque — became a magnificent example of French Gothic architecture. In the following period secular buildings such as city halls, residences, city fortifications and castles increased in significance alongside the churches.

Outstanding in intellectual history is the 1210 translation of the old Celtic saga of *Tristan and Isolde* by Gottfried von Strassburg. Several decades earlier the Abbess Gerrad von Idilienberg had composed her famous *Hortus Deliciarum*, which provides a unique overview of the state of knowledge at that time.

The development of the printing press and movable type, several centuries later,

The Romanesque abbey church of Marmoutier

View from the cathedral: Strasbourg old and new

allowed for the dissemination of works by the humanists of the Upper Rhine, such as Martin Buber, Beatus Rhenanus – the founder of the Humanist Library in Sélestat – and Jacob Sturm, the founder of Strasbourg's Latin School, which is considered the forerunner of the University. The beginning of the 16th century saw the creation of one of the masterpieces of the Middle Ages, Matthias Grünewald's Isenheim Altar. Until 1510, Geiler von Kayserberg agitated church officials with his sermons on the deplorable state of affairs in church and society. Earlier, in 1494, Sebastian Brant had ridiculed the folly of his time in *Ship of Fools*. From the 16th century on, Rennaisance architectural influences began to mix with those of the Gothic. An example of 18th-century neoclassical architecture is the Notre Dame Church in Guebwiller.

Today visitors come to the Alsace from all over the globe. What is less well known is that certain Alsatians have also managed to take their gifts out to the wider world. The Statue of Liberty in New York was created by the Colmar sculptor Frédéric Auguste Bartholdi. Hans Arp was also an Alsatian, and Tomi Ungerer, the famous artist and illustrator of childrens' books, was born in Strasbourg. The geographic location of Alsace may have lead to many bitter experiences down the years, but these have never managed to break the creative power and spirit of the native people.

Historical Outline

BC

100 Alsace is a Celtic region, home to the Sequans.

58 Caesar, called upon by the Sequans for help, is victorious over the invading Germanic Suebens led by Arovist.

52 Caesar puts down the rebellion of the Gauls under Vercingerotrix, with whom the Sequans had formed an alliance. For five centuries Alsace remains part of the Roman Empire.

12 Foundation of Argentoratum, the future Strasbourg.

AD

277 The Romans abolish laws restricting wine-production. Invasion of the Alemannians.

357 Emperor Julian secures the boundaries of the Empire by attacking the Alemannians at Strasbourg. However, by this stage, the Roman Empire is in decline.

From 406 Ever more frequent invasions by ancient Germanic tribes; the Alemanians settle in the Alsace.

7th–8th centuries The Alsace is a duchy within France. The founding of monasteries such as Murbach takes place.

842 Oath of Strasbourg: the famed oath of alliance between Ludwig the German and Karl the Bald against their brother Lothar is sworn. The first contract is drawn up in Old French and Old High German.

870 Alsace falls to Ludwig the German.

925 Alsace becomes part of the Duchy of Swabia and is later awarded to the Hohenstauffens.

1268 After the end of the Hohenstauffen reign Alsace disintegrates into a number of small principalities. City-republics arise.

1354 The Decapolis, an alliance of ten Alsatian cities is founded. The members are Colmar, Haguenau, Wissembourg, Obernai, Rosheim, Sélestat, Kayserberg, Turckheim, Munster and Mulhouse.

1439 Completion of the spire of Strasbourg cathedral; it remained the tallest building in Christendom until the 19th century.

16th century The Reformation extends through Alsace. Strasbourg and Sélestat become centres of humanism. Farmers' rebellions are bloodily suppressed. Grünewald paints the Issenheim altar, a masterpiece of medieval art.

1648 After Alsace suffered heavily in the Thirty Years' War, under the Peace of Westphalia the Habsburgs turn over their possessions in Alsace to the King of France.

1681 Alsace falls ever further under French rule when Strasbourg is annexed.

1870–1 The French lose the Franco-Prussian War and are forced to hand over Alsace and part of Lorraine to Germany.

1918 After World War I and heavy fighting in Alsace (the front line), Alsace becomes French again under the terms of the Treaty of Versailles.

1940 The Nazis occupy France and incorporate Alsace into the German Reich; men from Alsace-Lorraine are coerced into the German Wehrmacht and most of them are sent to the Russian Front.

1945 Alsace is French again.

1949 Strasbourg becomes the seat of the European Council and thus a symbol of French-German reconciliation.

LES VINS D'ALSACE
FRUCHTIG TROCKEN

Wine &

Inspired and Passionate

"A soft bosom and an tender hand has the Alsace, but it keeps its soul hidden – pulls away from the rapid grasp"; thus runs poet André Weckman's description of his home. André can well speak this way, since from his valley in the Vosges – just a cat's jump away from the *Route du Vin* – he can enjoy his Alsatian paradise without being knocked over by streams of tourists or having his mood ruined. The poet is one of the advocates – they have become rare – of an independent Alsatian culture. However, many others strongly support the *Elsässerdütch* dialect – which is ever more on the defensive against the use of French. When Germans cross the Rhine they feel almost at home with the language, though for an 'interior' Frenchman Alsace seems almost typically German. On the other hand, German visitors already believe themselves immersed in the French *esprit* when they journey between the Rhine and the Vosges. Thus Alsatians can woo you doubly – but they also feel divided inside. Sometimes they feel trapped by bureaucracy, because Paris is constantly taking pot-shots at Alsatian traditions.

When André Weckmann speaks of the hidden Alsatian soul, he doesn't mean the girls in traditional garb who sit by the fountain in Riquewihr and amplify the impression that the better part of

Traditional dress

Ceramics

the enchanting stretch of land along the *Route du Vin* is an open-air museum. Such a tipsy, folkloric dream world is found in many of the winemaking villages between Wissembourg, Strasbourg, Colmar and Mulhouse but right next door things are more cosy, vibrant and natural – more Alemannian.

Ribeauvillée on the Route du Vin

Alsatian Wine: Sampling Delirium.

The basic prerequisite for a full appreciation of the Alsatian 'wine route' is a refined nose. On the *Route du Vin* a real migration seems underway, especially at weekends. Migrants are lured by well-scrubbed wine-tasting rooms and wine cellars and they are attracted, as if to a magnet, by the typical *flûtes* – packed in cartons which are designed to resemble half-timbered houses – the perfect folkloristic turn-on. In order to discover 'your' vintner, a little excursion off the *Route du Vin* and into the villages and side-roads can be thoroughly rewarding. You only have to follow the signs saying '*Vente et Degustation*' to land in a cosy place where the vintner's family fills up the sampling glasses and conducts small talk with the customers – in German, Alsatian and French.

About what? Mostly about wine, naturally enough. Professsional oenologists have ferreted out the scent-composition of the prime Alsatian vintages. Wine testers have determined that the bouquet is composed – depending on the variety of grape, location and method of cultivation – of the scent of roses, hyacinths, acacias, violets, hawthorns, cinnamon, musk, honeysuckle, mignonette and a number of minerals!

Three varieties of wine grape are famed as specialities of the Alsace: Riesling, Gewürztraminer and Edelzwicker. Beyond these wine lovers also prize Silvaner, Pinot blanc, Pinot gris (which is also offered as Tokay d'Alsace) and Muscat. The **Edelzwicker** – a blend of noble grape varieties – is especially popular among Germans. I like to drink it with food as a light table wine, with a plate of sauerkraut, for example. The dry **Sylvaner** goes very well with fish and seafood of all kinds; the best of this wine is found in the Baar and Rouffach regions. A fish meal is also nicely rounded off with a fresh **Pinot blanc.** It is no coincidence that Alsatian white wine is prized on many of the coasts of France.

Without any doubt the crown belongs to the **Riesling**. It isn't difficult to lapse into rapture when you roll a dry, fruity and robust Riesling around your palate and get a thorough appreciation of its full flavour. The outstanding Riesling areas, including the Grand Crus, are found in the central section of the wine route, in other words Riquewihr, Zellenberg, Hunawihr, Ribbeauvillé and Dambach. A good sip of Riesling washes down fish nicely and brings an *hors d'oeuvre* to its full development; you can also drink it alone for a bit of merriment, without paying too heavily for it next morning.

Muscat – the best areas are Riquewihr and Ribbeauvillé – doesn't quite stand up to a comparison with the Rieslings, but certainly doesn't need to hide its face, especially when accompanying cheese. It's a bit sweeter than its noble cousin. In the neighbouring growing area of Baden, rosé wines are called *Weissherbst*; in the Alsace the Burgundy grape, fermented without the skin, produces wines arriving on the table as **Pinot gris** or **Tokay d'Alsace.** The fine, unmistakably spicy bouquet of a Pinot gris with its rosy blush shimmering in your glass is an outstanding match for all kinds of meat

Locally produced

Sample before buying

dishes and it makes an excellent accompaniment to the region's excellent fowl and wild game dishes.

I consider the **Gewürztraminer** as the wine which towers above the rest for the broadest variety of occasions. This Alsatian speciality goes just as well with *pâté de foie gras* as it does with dessert or cheeses; of course it is equally well-suited as a conversation-stimulant with your friends or as an apéritif. The Gewürztraminers are more or less dry depending on the location and the vintner and are among the *vins d'Alsace* with a higher alcohol content. The reason why so many wine lovers find what they are looking for between Guebwiller (Haut-Rhin) and Barr (Bas-Rhin) is connected with the genuine taste of Alsatian products. M J Dreyer, treasurer of the oldest French vintners' association, the Confrérie Saint-Etienne in Colmar, proudly emphasises: "Great pains are taken during the growing and pressing of the grapes to achieve the right balance between alcohol content, acidity and fruitiness." Thus the fruity, refreshing taste of the grapes comes to its full development and reaches the consumer as well. Marketing problems are unknown to Alsatian wine makers and vintners' associations, quite in contrast to some of the producers next door in Germany.

Alsatian wine is exported, of course, but it is a lot more fun to do your tasting and buying directly from the producers along the *Route du Vin*. One tip: wine in one-litre bottles should not be stored for longer than one year; for longer-term storage the wine offered in the *flûtes* (containing three-quarters of a litre) are better suited. After transporting, they should first be allowed to settle for several months before they are served – chilled, but not ice-cold. The best temperature range for Alsatian white wines is 7–9°C (43–48°F). To your health!

Ceramic as Souvenir

If you want to give a member of your family or a friend the unexpected pleasure of a souvenir that is both sensible and typically Alsatian, then in Soufflenheim and Betschdorf you will find an overwhelming selection. In both of these ceramic 'capitals' the visitor can acquire practical crockery which is especially appropriate to the decor of a rustic kitchen.

The stoneware tradition of Betschdorf has roots extending back to the ceramic craftsmen of the Westerwald who settled on the edge of the Haguenau Forest. Their speciality was a blue-grey earthenware – and this blue-grey glazing has remained a Betschdorf trademark up to the present day. In the family-run workshops an old division of labour is still prevalent: the men process the clay, sit at the potter's wheel and handle the kiln, while the women attach the handles, decorate the vessels and paint them. The decorative patterns are passed on from generation to generation and keep secret from competitors.

In Betschdorf – an excellent potters' centre which is full of half-timbered houses – there are several addresses worthy of recommendation for the purchase of waterproof stoneware (one especially practical idea stems from the fact that in a stoneware pitcher, wine stays fresh and remains unaltered in its taste). Pitchers, and many other sorts of vessel, can be had at the Poterie Schmitter (18 Rue

de la Poste) or at the shop of Gräs d'Alsace Schmitter-Burger (43 Rue des Poitiers), to name just two examples.

Soufflenheim displays considerably more competition. Perhaps your taste is more drawn to warm earthy tones and a greater variety of forms? At any rate the potters — male and female — at the numerous workshops in this town have their hands completely full in their efforts to supply the demands of tourists. Popular items are Dutch ovens, milk jugs, egg cups and escargot plates. Nowadays these earthenware items are mass-produced but painted, piece by piece, afterwards — you are guaranteed that the decoration is applied by hand, so each piece is unique. You can obtain a comprehensive list of addresses of the Soufflenheim workshops in the information office next door to the church. Two suggested addresses are Poterie d'Alsace Henri Siegfried (1É Rue de Haguenau) and Poterie Ludwig (9 Rue des Pierres and 5 Rue des Poitiers).

In northern Alsace, which in no way competes with the south, either in the beauty of its landscape or in its general prosperity, the pottery industry of these two villages has contributed to a certain prosperity. The foreign visitor armed with credit cards, dollars or pounds will find plenty of unusual souvenirs as well as useful kitchen items.

The Castle Romance of the Northern Vosges

A day-tour through the forests of the North Vosges Regional Park to the picture-book castles characteristic of the area.

The quaint little city of **Wissembourg** represents a good starting point for our excursion. It is located directly south of the French-German border in the broad basin of the Lauter river valley, only 10km (6 miles) distant from Bad Bergzabern. From the parking area on the edge of the city centre, the visitor need only take a few strides to get to the local historic showpieces, among which the Gothic church of Saint-Pierre-et-Saint-Paul is clearly the most outstanding. Between the Lauter and the city walls you will come across Renaissance buildings such as the **Haus des Ami Fritz** and the **Maison du Sel** with its characteristic roof. The terrace of the **Au Saumon** is an idyllic place for a glass of wine in the shade of the trees on the banks of the Lauter. There's a bit more bustle at

Wissembourg

the street cafés around the central Place de la République. 3km (2 miles) to the south of Wissembourg is the **Geisberg**, which should mean something to military historians: here, in 1870, the Battle of Weissenburg was fought, representing the bloody opening phase of the Franco-Prussian War.

From Wissembourg we now follow the direction signs to Bitche. The D3 road winds its way through the mixed forests of the North Vosges, which are about 400m (1,100 feet) in height. Their altitude bears no comparison to that of the South Vosges. If you want to make a really worthwhile stopover you will be well-pleased with the **Auberge du Cheval Blanc** in Lembach. Visitors from nearby Pirmasens are frequent guests in this restaurant and Alsatians prize the cuisine and ambience here.

Fleckenstein

Thus fortified we can venture an assault on the Fleckenstein castle ruins. The little road leading there branches off to the right 3km (2 miles) past Lembach. Those who want to combine a rest with an especially commanding view over the formidable castle walls should – at the next intersection – turn to the right again to the **Gimbelhof**. This restaurant, located on a high sunny plain directly on the border with the German state of Rheinland-Pfalz (Palatinate of the Rhineland), serves hearty rustic food in its garden; in its way a sort of *ferme-auberge* for the numerous hikers who pass this way.

Now let's head back and to the right – up to the Fleckenstein. It is enwrapped with tales (on this exposed spot how could it be otherwise?) and is one of the most astonishing ruins in the whole of Alsace. From a distance the viewer still cannot tell where the natural rock leaves off and where the walls begin. The castle-mountain – or mountain-castle, if you will – has as many holes in it as a Swiss cheese. It is great fun for children who creep stealthily around through the secret-laden passageways and imagine themselves to be knights on the observation platform: an adventure playground *par exellence*. Castle Fleckenstein originates from the 12th century and the ruins, which are merged with the native sandstone, present one of the most outstanding opportunities in the Alsace region to take a look at medieval methods of castle-building. Matthäus Nerian was also slain on these walls (in his day still intact) built on the steep cliffs. His copper engravings have made him and Fleckenstein famous.

Next we drive further west along the valley of the Lauter, and between Niedersteinbach and Obersteinbach (the finest of Alsatian specialities are served there in the **Restaurant Anthon**) we come upon the turn-off to Wasigenstein. Turn right here and, after a stretch of 2km (1.25 miles) with many good vantage points, you will come to a parking place in the forest; from there take the path to the ruins — a hike of about ten minutes. In spite of its romantic setting, **Wasigenstein** is overshadowed by the much more imposing Fleckenstein ruins. Even so, contemplating the ruins on each side of the steep gorge you can well imagine why the notorious duel from the Nibelungen legends took place in this forest.

The fact that this entire region was for centuries a disputed and much fought-over border area is evidenced by the numerous medieval castles in the North Vosges, and especially by the forbidding fortifications in and around **Bitche**. Here the absolutist spirit of the fortress master-builder Vauban predominates. His works can still be seen all over Alsace as well as in the neighbouring German region of Baden. Massive bastions encompass the citadel of Bitche and seem to be watching over the town in such a way that is not likely to inspire the visitor with a sense of romance. To me, the fortifications of Bitche seem rather frightening. It's a good thing that the Germans and the French have patched up their differences. So should we think of Bitche as a warning memorial to times gone by? That makes sense. And just like the Maginot Line, the Hartmanswillerkopf, the cemeteries of fallen soldiers and those of the Jews and the Struthof concentration camp, the citadel stands as a stony reminder that we should never again let discordant and murderous war break out among us.

We depart Bitche to the southwest in the direction of Sarreguemines and look for the direction sign (on the left-hand side of the D37) to **Lemberg** soon after. This little town is known for its crystal-glass products. Vases, glasses and all kinds of vessels are offered for sale in the shops and display rooms on both sides of the street that passes through the village. However, if you want to buy at the best prices you should go direct to the producer.

Just beyond the railway flyover at Lemberg we turn left onto the

Fortifications in Bitche

D36. Here you will find signs directing you to Baerenthal and Philipsbourg. I find this quiet section of the North Vosges especially pleasant: there is little traffic and the region's small villages stand in valley pastures surrounded by mixed forests. Here time seems almost to have stood still, and exactly because this landscape has such an unspectacular appearance, it radiates a rustic charm. Nothing represents better the leisurely pace of life here than the number of anglers, both young and old, who come to fish around the **Waldsee**. Fishing here is a family event and companionship plays as important a part as the catch, helped along by generous quantities of Kronenbourg beer or Molsheim Riesling.

Travelling through green forests alongside reddish-coloured sandstone cliffs we arrive at **Phillipsbourg**. Those fascinated with the magical romance of castles can turn to the left here towards **Falkenstein**. However, if you have had your fill of medieval castles, you should turn to the right on to the N62 highway. After 6km (3¾ miles) you can make a side trip to the healing baths of **Neiderbronn-les-Bains**. This place has been known since Roman times for its hot springs, although it does not radiate the 'fashionable' atmosphere which is typical of many such places. Nonetheless, with a remarkable restaurant (in the **Hotel Bristol** by the City Hall), a

Niederbronn-les-Bains

grand hotel, and the only **casino** in Alsace, Niederbronn has its attractions. Even Strasbourg cannot keep up with that.

From rural Niederbronn continue to Reichshoffen and then turn left to **Woerth**. This town is located in a gently rolling landscape and achieved sad fame through the Franco-Prussian War, just like Weissenburg Castle. This ivy-grown castle in the centre of the town houses a museum to the battle of 1870, and direction signs point the way to the **champ de bataille** – the battlefield.

Some visitors will be surprised to learn that Alsace was once one

Fishing at Bitche

of the oil-producing regions of the world. Only three decades ago prospectors drilled for black gold in **Pechelbronn**. The name of the town is derived from the oily pitch (*pech* in German) which, even in medieval times, was extracted and used as lubrication for wagon axles; it was later used for healing purposes as well. In the petroleum museum at Merckwiller-Pechelbronn (today a thermal spa-town) there are displays telling the story of the Alsatian oil boom. A few kilometres further to the east much more pleasant thoughts come our way in the quaint centre of Soultz-sous-Forêts. This town marks the beginning of the **northern Route du Vin**, not nearly as well-known as its sister route in the south. Even so, it is still an attractive route, passing through many an unspoiled village. In the middle of the region's fertile landscape, despite the intoxicating scenery, we are unfortunately not spared a view with a martial aspect to it: in **Schoenenbourg** the largest complex of fortifications in the Maginot Line can be examined. During World War II a gigantic barracks was constructed, complete with bunkers and fox-holes, and it was one of the most important French positions against the German Wehrmacht. The barracks at Schoe-nenbourg are now a primary tourist attraction and stand as a memorial to the Maginot Line;

On the Maginot Line

in the concrete bunkers the majority of visitors from both East and West still experience a shudder of horror at the thought of the waste and violence that was brought about by both World Wars.

Not far beyond Schoe-nenbourg a minor road branches off to the left from the D264 leading to **Hunspach**. At the entrance to the village there is a clear indication of why Hunspach is among the most beautiful villages in France: the geraniums in the windows are a most welcoming sign that in Hunspach the rustic world of northern Alsace is still in good order.

If you are running out of time, Wissembourg can be reached very swiftly along the well-improved D263. You could, however, make a detour in order to finish off this excursion much more pleasantly. A minor road leads westward out of Hunspach passing through Bremmelbach to **Cleebourg** – located in the heart of the Northern Alsatian Wine Route. Now a Cleebourger Pinot or a Riesling from this most northerly wine-producing county in Alsace would do just nicely, and in the **Restaurant à la Cave de Cleebourg** (Tel: 88 94 52 18; right next door to the central wine-cellar) the Alsatian culinary arts are represented especially well by a pheasant on a bed of sauerkraut.

Restaurants

Wissembourg

WINSTUB DU MUSEE
21 Rue des Juifs.
Tel: 88 94 00 97.
Closed Wednesday evening and Thursday.
A cosy wine-tavern with regional cooking; medium prices.

Lembach

LE CHEVAL BLANC
4 Rue de Wissembourg.
Tel: 88 94 41 86.
Closed Monday and Tuesday.
One of the best restaurants in northern Alsace featuring regional specialities, particular noted for its cuisine, prepared masterfully by Fernand Mischler with his 18-strong kitchen team. The prices correspond to the quality and the ambience.

FERME DU GIMBELHOF
Towards the Fleckenstein ruins.
Tel: 88 94 43 59.
Closed Monday and Tuesday.
A mountain guest house including a rustic restaurant and garden service with a good view; reasonable overnight accomodation.

Niederbronn-les-Bains

LES ACACIAS
35 Rue des Acacias.
Tel: 88 09 00 47.
Closed Friday and Saturday afternoon.
A relaxing atmosphere despite the large dining room. Regional cuisine and wild game specialities; moderate prices.

Hotels

Wissembourg

LE CYGNE
3 Rue du Sel.
Tel: 88 94 00 16.
Rooms: £20–30.

Niederbronn-les-Bains

BRISTOL
4 Place de l'Hotel-de-Ville.
Tel: 88 09 61 44.
Rooms: £17.50–27.50.

South of Haguenau

Clay Creations

Potters' villages, Goethe's first love, Rhine idyll and the Haguenau Forest.

As far as landscape goes, this route doesn't have the same drama as the Wine Route or the Vosges. Instead, today we are going to concentrate on gentler pleasures; with the workshops of Alsatian potters, with an orgy of half-timbered buildings in the plain of the Rhine and with the amorous adventures of the poetic genius, Goethe. The point of departure for this roundtour is **Haguenau**, located about half-an-hour north of Strasbourg by car. Haguenau can be reached by way of Route Nationale 63, passing by industrial complexes and the suburbs of the Alsatian metropolis, but also going through the hilly extension of

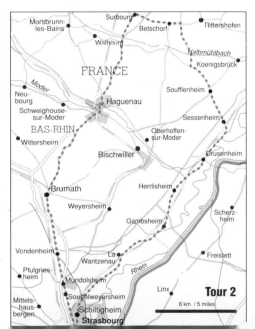

Flags flying in Haguenau

the fertile Kochersberger region.

Haguenau itself is not one of the most attractive of Alsatian towns. The ravages of the Thirty Years' War, plundering by the French in the 17th century and, above all, Allied bomb attacks in the Second World War have destroyed the greatest part of the medieval city, which was once the main city of the Ten City Alliance (the Decapolis), the location of the imperial palace and ringed by a city wall which included 40 towers. Today there is nothing to be seen of this, so a tour through the city can concentrate on two churches: **St Georges** is in the centre and its art treasures include an altar wing inspired by Schongauer. We find **St Nicolas** on the road out towards Wissembourg, it dates to the 12th century, the time of Frederick I (Barbarossa). The saint's grave with its Gothic tracery and sculpture is the highlight of the church.

Museum fans will find two noteworthy examples for their study: the **Alsatian Museum** (Place Thierry) displays Alsatian folk-art, and the **Historical Museum** (Rue Maréchal-Foch) has exhibits from prehistory to the present day. Since we are in the city of the once-famous imperial palace, it would be appropriate to recommend **Le Kaiserhof** among the restaurants in Haguenau. The city is also one of the most important Alsatian centres of the brewer's art; there is an annual hop-festival in mid-August, when a wealth of cultural presentations take place throughout the city centre.

Not far beyond the St Nicolas church and the bridge over the Moder the road forks. We remain on the D263 heading in the direction of Wissembourg and wind up right in the middle of the Forêt de Haguenau – the Haguenau Forest – which is a true paradise for hikers and cyclists with its abundance of paths forging through dense woods.

Where the Haguenau Forest gives way to farmland and pastures, the D243 branches off to the right – towards **Betschdorf**. There are few towns anywhere that have as many houses of half-timbered construction as in Betschdorf: there must be hundreds of them bordering both sides of the main road through the town. They provide an appropriate setting for the pottery workshops which have been a tradition in Betschdorf for centuries. Frederick Barbarossa granted the potters the perpetual right to continue their

historic practice of mining clay from the rich deposits in the Haguenau Forest. Thus the stoneware of Betschdorf, with its characteristic blue glaze, has a long history. The production and decoration of the blue-grey stoneware can be observed in several of the pottery workshops. Naturally, there is also more than sufficient opportunity for you to purchase pots, pitchers and bowls directly from the producers (see *Ceramic as Souvenir* for some addresses).

Soufflenheim has considerably fewer half-timbered buildings than Betschdorf, but the number of tourists coming here substantially exceeds those visiting the neighbouring village. The main reason for this lies in the fact that the ceramics of Soufflenheim are regarded as the embodiment of traditional Alsatian design. Earthy tones with colourful flower ornamentation grace the escargot pans, Dutch ovens, crinoline pitchers, bowls and wine jugs.

Try and park your car in the area near the **church**, next door to which is housed the **Tourist Information Office**. There you can obtain the addresses of the four pottery workshops in Soufflenheim that allow you to watch over the shoulders of the men operating the wheels and the women painting the vessels (see also *Ceramic as Souvenir* for some addresses). Although the display windows and exhibition rooms contain many kitsch articles, traditional forms and colours predominate. And – in my entirely personal opinion

Geraniums and half-timbering; an Alsatian speciality

— bread stays fresher in a Soufflenheim stoneware bowl with a lid than by any other storage method.

During the time he spent studying law in Strasbourg, Goethe was not much interested in pottery; nor, for the matter, did he have much time for literature, law, Gothic architecture or Alsatian cuisine — he only had eyes for Friederike Brion. This parson's daughter lived in Sesenheim — today spelt **Sessenheim**. This little town is located 4km (2.5 miles) south of Soufflenheim and, since the Alsatians know how greatly the German people revere their poetic prince, the Sessenheimers have transformed this place, where the romance between the young Goethe and Friederike was played out, into a modest tourist attraction. Thus you can examine a little **Goethe Memorial** on the main street and join fans flocking to the **Auberge du Boeuf** (Inn of the Oxen). The host has lovingly created a mini-museum in a side room where he displays letters and writings gathered from the time when the young Goethe rode on horseback from Strasbourg University into the sleepy little Rhine Valley village of Sesenheim.

The return route through this section of the Bas-Rhin to Strasbourg can be purgatory during the commuter rush-hour, so try to avoid doing it in the early evening. The D300 takes you quickly to the outlying districts of Strasbourg. The residential blocks and industrial parks give no hint that the historical centre of a medieval imperial city is only a short distance away. We drive past one side of the modern **Palais d'Europe** on our way. When the flags of the EC member states are flying it means that the European Parliament is meeting in its impressive council hall.

Restaurants

Haguenau

BARBEROUSSE
8 Place Barberousse.
Tel: 88 73 31 09.
Closed Sunday evening and Monday.
Hearty regional cuisine; in summer there is a beautiful and quiet dining-terrace; moderate prices.

La Wantzenau

ZIMMER
23 Rue des Héros.
Tel: 88 96 20 23.
Closed Sunday evening and Monday.
Already within the metropolitan area of Strasbourg, this is a genuine traditional restaurant with the emphasis on classic Alsatian cuisine; moderate prices.

Hotels

La Wantzenau

HOTEL DU MOULIN
23 Route de Strasbourg.
Tel: 88 96 27 83.
A quiet hotel in an old mill outside the half-timbered village of La Wantzenau. An excellent place for staying overnight when visiting Strasbourg. A room costs £25–35.

The neighbouring restaurant of the same name, offers gourmet dishes while 'Mére Clauss' offers specialities such as duck salad and fish dishes in the upper price range.

TOUR ③

Through the North Vosges Mountains

Cliffs, castles, forests and fields around Saverne.

Crossing the Saverne Pass is, depending on how you look at it, like going through the eye of a needle, or the most comfortable passage over the Vosges. For centuries, due to its topography, the **Col de Saverne** has served as a gateway, a place for troop formation and deployment, and a recreation area. Here the North Vosges are only 4km (2.5 miles) wide and some 410m (1,345ft) high and from the top of the pass a good road winds down to **Saverne**, which was named *Tres Tabernae* (Three Taverns) by the Romans.

Saverne

Saverne has several guest-houses in its easily explored old quarter, and the terrace of the **Taverne Katz**, in front of the finely carved half-timbered house (in the Grand'Rue pedestrian zone) is among the most popular meeting places here.

The best starting-point for a stroll around the 'Rose City of Saverne' (so called because of the rose-pink colour of the local granite) is the parking area in front of the **Château des Rohan** – the Rohan Castle. This 18th-century building, in neoclassical style,

Château des Rohan, Saverne

turns its most photogenic side toward the Rhine-Marne Canal. Even though the park between the magnificent facade and the shoreline area seems a bit scruffy, it is worth taking a few strides around this 'Alsatian Versailles'. During the 18th century the Prince-Bishop of Strasbourg resided here; today there are government agencies, a youth hostel and a historical museum (the **Musée National**, open from 2–6pm) sheltered within the castle.

Directly adjacent to the parking area is a **carousel**, which makes a visit to the castle a big thrill for children. On Thursdays those who saunter over to the large **marketplace** on the Place Général de Gaulle will see and taste what a bountiful garden the Rhine

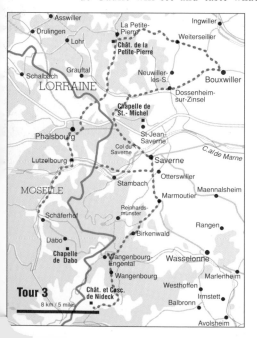

river plain east of Saverne is. From there you can also take in the pleasures of the Rose Garden (**La Roseraie** on the Rue de Paris; west of the Rohan Castle). There are well over 1,000 varieties of roses to delight the visitor from June to September (open weekdays from 10am–7pm).

One of the most outstanding observation points in the region can be reached in just a few minutes from Saverne: **Haut-Barr** is appropriately called the 'Eye of Alsace'. Here castle ruins tower over the entire region to the southwest of Saverne; on gangways and wooden staircases you can clamber from rock to rock and admire the farsightedness of the Prince-Bishops of Strasbourg, who had their summer residence constructed on this eagle's eyrie – high above their subjects and the world – in 1170.

Next we depart from Saverne in the direction of Sarre-Union and, roughly half-way up the heavily forested **Saverne Pass**, we come upon the **Jardin Botanique** (Botanic Garden), which is well worth a visit. A short way beyond the top of the pass the D122 branches off to the right towards La Petite Pierre and the Parc Vosges du Nord. At the next intersection we turn half-right in the direction of Bouxwiller. The road leads through the forests of the North Vosges and finally enters the hilly and fertile landscape around **Bouxwiller**, an attractive little town which is not overrun with tourists. Following the direction signs to La Petite Pierre and Ingwiller, we join the **D7**. Like most French country roads, the traffic on this route is minimal, making our drive through quiet villages, forests and valleys even more enjoyable.

Just where the D7 begins to ascend, the **Castle La Petite Pierre** appears, located almost within arm's reach – a high point of the day. In this little vacation town the road branches off to the right towards the château; the shady plaza has room for parking and the snack-booth sells delicious crêpes. Nowadays the information office of the **North Vosges Natural Park** is housed in the Lützelstein –

La Petite Pierre

the castle's original name. This *parc naturel* extends in the shape of a semicircle from Saverne to Wissembourg and in the north turns – without interruption – into the Pfälzerwald Natural Park in Germany. To the west it forms the border between Alsace and Lorraine. The view from the battlements of the Lützelstein ruins does

View from Dabo

not reach that far, but the outlook is impressive nonetheless. Furthermore, you can imagine how Jerrihans – the legendary Count of the Palatinate – was inspired, in his eagle-eyrie in this forest world, to draw up his social policies for the region.

Our next destination is named **Phalsbourg**. After we have driven down the mountain from La Petite Pierre, a little river winds along between the green cliffs. We turn to the left towards Oberhof at the next intersection and then, not much further on, we turn off to the right towards Phalsbourg. The military leaders of past centuries made this town their base and built tremendous bastions, the remains of which you can still see today. Considering the strategic significance of Phalsbourg it is no wonder that in the centre of the expansive marketplace a bronze officer keeps watch.

Before we leave Phalsbourg why not sample a *café au lait* in one of the numerous pavement cafés here. Heading out from the inner city we head first in the direction of Sarrebourg then, almost immediately, branch off to the left towards Lutzelbourg and Dabo.

At **Lutzelbourg** we are not so much interested in the castle, but rather in a more recent technical masterpiece. On the Rhine-Marne Canal, to the west of Lutzelbourg on the D98, you can look in awe at a ship hoist (*Plan incliné de St Louis-Arzviller*) which transports ships by means of an inclined elevator over a height difference of more than 100m (358ft). Not far beyond this is a 3-km (2-mile) long ship tunnel to astonish us. Both of these attractions are unique in France and, if you ask, you can usually get a ride on board a ship as it passes through the tunnel. The canal is nearly always busy with the traffic of motorboats and freight barges. The Rhine-Marne Canal also has a cycle path alongside it – travelling the length of the canal makes for a thoroughly exciting vacation.

Already visible from far away is the **Rock of Dabo**, a mountaintop lookout point. If you drive up the ring-shaped road that leads to the Rocher de Dabo and climb up the stairs to the observation platform on the tower of the chapel, you will have all of Alsace at your feet. The chapel was erected in honour of Leo IX, the only Alsatian pope. His name before being elected pope was Bruno von Dagsburg. It is best not to drive up to the Rock at weekends as the crush of tourists can detract from the beautiful view.

The Rhine-Marne Canal

Having returned from St Leon to the main road, we now turn to the right towards Wasselone. The **Forests of the North Vosges** are strongly reminiscent of the Northern Black Forest across the river, and there are numerous paths marked out for hiking. One of the most beautiful leads to the romantic ruins of the **Castle Nideck** with its thundering waterfall. Access to this side-excursion from our tour branches off past Obersteigen from the D45 – a worthwhile complement to the day. As an alternative to natural spectacles, **Marmoutier** is a tradition-rich town with a wonderful church, once part of a Benedictine abbey. The fountain in the marketplace of Marmoutier is a good spot for viewing the symmetrical west facade of the Romanesque **abbey church** – or the 'Castle of God'. In the nave of the church a fine Silbermann organ is contrasted with painted glass and ashlar blocks of reddish sandstone, which appear well-proportioned despite their size. Those interested in Romanesque architecture in its pure form will find Marmoutier an examplary model.

A well-improved road takes us back to Saverne, our starting point. In the **Zawermer Stuebel** (Rue des Fréres) let the excitement and fatigue of the day give way to relaxation as we partake of the restaurant's Alsatian specialities and wines.

Restaurants and Hotels

Saverne

TAVERNE KATZ
80 Grand'Rue.
Tel: 88 71 16 56.
Closed Tuesday and Wednesday afternoon.
A picture-book wine bar with a culinary tradition: Alsatian regional cuisine of the finest preparation; menu prices start at £15.

La Petite Pierre

HOTEL DES VOSGES
30 Rue Principal.
Tel: 88 70 45 05.
Closed Tuesday evening and Wednesday.
A traditional house with a large selection of dishes on its menu. This family-run business has a home-like atmosphere – and a touch of luxury. Rooms cost £25 45.

LE LION D'OR
15 Rue Principale.
Tel: 88 70 45 06.
Closed Wednesday evening and Thursday.
Hearty country fare with gourmet ambitions (wild-game dishes, filet of sole) and a complete children's menu for £4.50. Also, a modernised hotel with sports facilities in an idyllic location. Rooms cost £20–40.

Phalsbourg

LE SOLDAT DE L'AN II
1 Rue de Saverne.
Tel: 87 24 16 16.
Closed Sunday evening and Monday.
One of the best addresses on the Mosel – located in a historic building. Chef Georges Schmidt will surprise you with his creativity: among his colleagues he is considered one of the best. His exquisite cuisine has its price: *Menus complêtes* start at around £40.

Strasbourg's Most Beautiful Side

Through the city's old quarter: the Cathedral to Petite France.

If you are looking for a quiet corner for some contemplation in the Strasbourg Cathedral, you won't have much luck during the tourist season. At that time an endless stream of art lovers and curious sightseers fills the very last nook of this immense temple. The cathedral is a towering monument – figuratively and literally. It is not only the major sight in Alsace, it is also one of the top-ranking sights in all of Europe. Motorists arriving before 9am will almost certainly find a parking place in one of the numerous parking lots or underground garages in the area of the old city – parking doesn't become a problem until later on. Visitors with a weak command of French might have problems deciphering what they are supposed to do at some of the ticket machines. There is, however, no great secret: the keyboard is there for the purpose of entering your car's registration number, which is printed on the ticket after you have paid (eight francs for two hours).

Every visitor to Strasbourg gravitates towards the **Place de la Cathédral**. I am constantly fascinated by the contrasting scene which greets you when you come from Place Gutenberg. Rue Mercière is a souvenir paradise – doing complete justice to its name, which means 'Merchant Street' – and whenever you lift your gaze over the postcard stands and balloons you catch sight of the over-

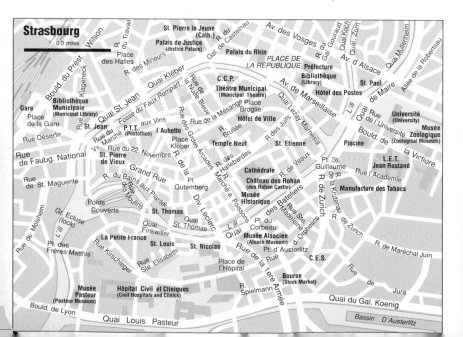

Strasbourg cityscape

whelming west façade of the cathedral. During the summer the Place de la Cathédral looks more like a stage – an animated playground full of street musicians, jugglers, portrait painters, clowns and actors competing to attract attention – and to attract francs (or whatever currency you have). In the pavement cafés tourists enjoy the ambience and liquid refreshments – at juicy prices.

The crowning glory of the west façade of the cathedral is the **Rose Window**, which has a diameter of 15m (50ft). Before contemplating this gleaming example of glass-painting from the interior of the cathedral, it is worthwhile, first, to make a detailed examination of the **stone sculptures** of the three portals. To prevent these prophets, apostles and virgins from continuing erosion by acid rain, the cathedral authorities have had almost all of the original 13th-century statues replaced with replicas. The cathedral shelters a wealth of art treasures, among them an angel-ornamented column, the stone pulpit, a Silbermann organ and the stained-glass windows. At 12.30pm there is always a crush of people around the 19th-century **astronomical clock** – this is the time at which the fine mechanism, with its apostles, star-signs and angels, comes to life.

If you have the energy for it, try climbing the 330 steps to the **Cathedral's platform**. The staircase starts next to the cashier's booth (business hours: 8.30am–7pm). In the mornings and evenings especially, the old quarter of Strasbourg, seen from a bird's eye perspective, looks like an untouched town from a bygone

Rose window, Strasbourg cathedral

Strasbourg cathedral's west façade

century. However, it is equally evident – from 66m (220ft) up – that the clocks haven't stood still in this old imperial city: neoclassical town-houses, palatial Wilhelminian buildings, and the rectangular 'dwelling machines' of the most recent decades as well as the towering administration and bank buildings of the present day extend beyond the half-timbered romanticism at our feet.

The construction of the cathedral began in the 11th century, and the building and/or renovation of this mammoth structure continues to the present. It is almost beyond imagining how our ancestors managed to construct the 142m (465ft) tower using only muscle power – as well as a wealth of imagination. However, the architects knew their technological ropes. Once the exterior sandstone walls were erected using wooden scaffolding, a huge wooden wheel was installed in the windy heights, wide enough for several people to run around the treadmill – thus raising the heavy stones by winch lines.

After so much culture we've earned a rest. Why not spend some time in the **Maison Kammerzell**, the magnificent merchant's house on the south side of the cathedral plaza? In the stone-built ground floor is a wine-bar; the half-timbered first floor shelters an elegant restaurant. The boutiques and art galleries on the **Rue des Hallebardes** – into which we make a right turn – radiate their own special atmosphere. From here we go left into the **Rue du Dome**, which is equally loaded with shops and has a tourist information office. **Place Broglie**, with its heavy traffic, is framed by the city theatre (Opera du Rhin), the Banque de France and the old City Hall. Now we turn left into **Rue des Mésang** to arrive at the **Place Kleber**, a traffic roundabout with a bronze statue of a general and a merry-go-round for the children. Also located here – as in the **Rue des Grandes Arcades** – are department stores, travel agencies, speciality shops and cafés in great number. This arcade street empties into the **Place Gutenberg**, where a stone monument commemorates the inventor of moveable type for printing presses. He laid the groundwork for the dissemination of humanistic thought – a fact which has had considerable impact on Strasbourg. Housed in the **Hôtel du Commerce** is a tourist office with a plethora of brochures awaiting you. From here **Petite France** is only a couple of minutes away by foot. The orgy of half-timbered buildings here in the **Tanners' Quarter** is more reminiscent of a romantic Old Germany. The name of this idyllic Strasbourgeoise high temple of tourism is not as romantic as it seems; it derives from the former Hospital Petite France (named after the French designation for syphilis – the so-called 'Frenchman's disease').

Now we follow the direction signs through the narrow **Rue de Serruriers**, arriving at the **Rue de la Monnaie**, the **Thomasplatz** and the **Rue du Bain-aux-Plantes**. Around the overcrowded and picturesque **Place Benjamin Six**, the pulse of anyone who loves half-timbered buildings, sauerkraut, goose liver and Riesling wine will quicken a little. There you will find one wine-tavern after another; little restaurants with homely names (Chéz Tante Liesel, for example) offer cosy atmosphere and Alsatian specialities. Their distinguishing feature is overflowing floral decorations and red-and-white chequered tablecloths. One of the most beautiful of the garden-cafés in Petite France is **Aux Petit Bois Vert**.

The half-timbered façade of the **Gerwerstub** harmonises with the shady trees along the riverbank, the scent of sauerkraut lingers in your nose and rumbling in front of your eyes are excursion boats that slide gently past on the River Ill; a stream of visitors comes swarming off the little swing-bridge onto the **Rue des Moulins**: a doll's-house fantasy *en gros et en detail*.

Past the Ill bridge, at the end of the Rue du Bain-aux-Plantes, the old quarter comes to an abrupt end; we turn half-left across the large market place to the **Ponts Couverts** – the covered bridges. These casemates are the work of Général Vauban, whose military-architectural legacy all over Alsace is impossible to overlook. Fortunately, in Strasbourg the fortification has been turned into an observation platform from which you can best survey Little France with the four Ill canals and the façade of the cathedral in the background. By the way, in the passageway of the **Barrage Vauban** you can also see a number of sculptures from the cathedral.

From the Ponts Couvert we proceed along the Ill to the **Rue des Moulins**. A glimpse from the bridge back to Petite France makes

The River Ill and the Ponts Couverts

Waiting for business in the Place de la Cathédral

clear once again the attractiveness of this 'open-air museum' with its half-timbered buildings, navigable waterways and an incredible number of garden-cafés. Nearby is another particularly attractive address: the **Restaurant Pont St Martin** (located by the restaurant's namesake) which has tables alongside and even over the Ill. Back at the **Rue de la Monnaie**, turn to the right to **Quai St Thomas**. The church of St Thomas dates to the early 13th century. The tomb of Moritz von Sachsen is among the noteworthy things in the interior of the church. Albert Schweitzer played the Silbermann organ in this church to gather donations for his clinic in Africa.

At the Ill our path turns to the left; along the riverside walkways we saunter past residences representative of the Belle Epoque on our way back to the heart of the old quarter. Between the Ill and the cathedral we come across Strasbourg's **Museum Quarter**. Folk-art has its home in the Musée Alsacien; the Musée Historique tells the story of the city's turbulent history; art exhibitions are offered at the Musée d'Art Moderne in the former Ancienne Douane (Customs House).

The **Château des Rohan** provides its visitors with several interesting museums: the splendid 18th-century Grands Appartements on the ground floor convey an aristocratic atmosphere; the Musée des Beaux

Arts (Museum of Fine Arts) on the floor above presents masterpieces from many centuries, including the *Schöne Strassburgerin*; and in the Archeological Museum you can examine the Roman remains of old *Argentoratum* (Strasbourg's original name). If you have not had your fill of history, the nearby Musée de l'Oeuvre Notre-Dame houses the documents, furniture and many original sculptures from the cathedral's west façade.

This last museum is located between the château and the Place de la Cathédral. I consider the neighbouring **Place du Marché aux Cochons de Lait** (Piglet Market) to be one of the most attractive places in the old quarter. Unfortunately, my opinion is shared by all-too-many Strasbourg fans, and thus the crush of tourists is correspondingly heavy. For this reason it is sometimes difficult to find a place to sit in the **Strissel**, the **Vogel Strauss** or in the **Pfifferbriader** so that you can enjoy a Pinot Blanc or a Strasbourger beer fresh from the barrel. Our excursion around the old quarter of Strasbourg is now finished but if you want to explore further it is more comfortable to experience the city centre in a **horse-drawn coach** or in the slow, old-fashioned trams (these start out at irregular intervals from the cathedral's north side).

A **boat-excursion** is particularly worth recommending. The *Promenade en Bateaux* lasts about one hour (embarcation and ticket sales at the Place du Marché aux Poissons right next to the Château des Rohan; price 30 francs for adults and 15 francs for children). Boats depart regularly between 9am and 9pm; they are shielded from bad weather by large domes, and loudspeaker announcements in three languages tell you about the various bridges, locks and buildings on both banks of the Ill.

The trip also includes a riverside view of Strasbourg's modern 'Europa' quarter and the **Palais de l'Europe**. This modern – almost futuristic – building is the seat of the European Council, the workplace of hundreds of officials and, one week per month, the meeting place of the European Parliament. If you are interested in politics you can watch the multilingual sessions of the European Parliament from the visitor's balcony (reservations: Service des Visites; Tel: 88 61 49 61). After the dry debates, a dry Alsatian wine tastes even better.

Romantic Petite France

Restaurants

LA MOUCHE
42 Rue Finckwiller.
Tel: 88 36 04 18.
Closed Sunday and Monday
A pleasant, cosy tavern on the edge of Petite France in which you can also eat good regional specialities at moderate prices.

MAISON DES TANNEURS
42 Rue du Bain-aux-Plantes.
Tel: 88 32 79 70.
Closed Sunday and Monday.
Picture-book backdrop with half-timber construction, geraniums and hand-crafted decorations in the heart of the Tanner's Quarter. Traditional Alsatian cuisine at international prices.

BISTRO DE LA GARE
18 Rue de Vieux-Marché-aux-Grains (by the Place Gutenberg).
Tel: 88 22 43 75.
Changing daily menu at reasonable prices.

LE TIRE-BOUCHON
5 Rue de Tailleurs-de-Pierre.
Tel: 88 32 47 86.
Closed Sunday and Monday afternoon.
One of Strasbourg's most beautiful wine-taverns with smaller and larger offerings of Alsatian cuisine.

CHEZ YVONNE
10 Rue de Sanglier.
Tel: 88 32 84 15.
Closed Sunday and Monday afternoon.
This old *Burjerstuewel* has developed under the management of Yvonne into one of the most friendly meeting places in Strasbourg. The menu extends from Munster cheese to the finest fish. With this the many guests drink the house wines.

LE BUEREHIESEL
4 Parc de l'Orangerie.
Tel: 88 61 62 24.
Closed Tuesday evening and Wednesday.
One of the five four-star restaurants in Strasbourg. In the glass extension you feel as if you are in a conservatory. This culinary temple certainly requires a well-padded wallet. However, true gourmets will find their pleasures here, with complete menus ranging from £30–50.

Le Crocodile
10 Rue de L'Outre.
Tel: 88 32 13 02.
Closed Sunday and Monday.
The renown of Chef Emile Jung
reaches far beyond the Alsatian
borders. *Nouvelle cuisine* came
to life, partly, here in the middle
of Old Strasbourg. Connoisseurs
will be delighted here with the
quality of the *pâte de fois gras*
(goose-liver paté), the fish and
the sorbets. The *menu de dégus-
tation* can easily swallow close
to £70 – that's per person –
not for a family of five.

Hotels

In this frequently booked-up
'Euro-city' there are hotels and
pensions *en masse* at all comfort
and price levels. Here are a few
suggestions:

Convent du Franciscain
18 Rue du Faubourg de Pierre.
Tel: 88 32 93 93.
Located near the city centre,
simple but comfortable. Rooms:
£20–30.

Le Gutenberg
31 Rue des Serruriers.
Tel: 88 32 17 15.
Central location at reasonable
prices. Rooms: £20 and up.

Le Dragon
2 Rue de l'Ecarlate.
Tel: 88 35 79 80.
Near the centre, a modern
house with comforts behind
an old façade. Rooms from
£35 upwards.

Cathedral-Dauphin
2 Place de la Cathédral.
Tel: 88 22 12 12.
Located directly by the

Cathedral. A quiet address for
the demanding – and well-heeled
– guest. Rooms start at £40.

Le Regent Contades
8 Avenue de la Liberté.
Tel: 88 36 26 26.
A luxury hotel for the *crème* of
the world of politics, business
and culture. Here you find not
just comfort, but a variety of
entertainment. Questions about
the price of an overnight stay
are irrelevant to most of the
guests, however for the rest of
us, rooms start at £65.

TOUR 5

Strasbourg After Sunset

For a real Alsatian the evening begins to take shape with an aperitif. Around 7pm – after work and before dinner – people meet with friends, acquaintances or colleagues for a couple of rounds. This tradition is sociable, helps you to relax and simultaneously puts you in the mood for the evening to come – when going out to eat is by far the most popular activity.

One of Strasbourg's best-known meeting-places is **Le Petit Maxim**, in the heart of the city near the Place Kléber (4 Place de l'Homme de Fer. Tel: 88 23 05 00; open daily). On the ground floor of this two-level restaurant (also a pizzeria) at around 7pm it is perfectly acceptable just to order drinks. The pina coladas – coconut milk spirit with pineapple juice – are excellent here. Le Petit Maxim is a comfortable place for lounging and enjoying the view over the 'Plaza of the Man of Iron' with its evening goings-on. If you like this restaurant you can chalk it up for the really late hours of the night, when, after dancing in the disco has worn you out, a sudden attack of hunger overwhelms you. Hot food is served in the Petit Maxim until 6am. This type of restaurant, providing the European metropolis with almost round-the-clock service, is relaxing and rarely overflows with customers.

You can get a better idea of the busy pace of Strasbourg's business life from the bar **Le Waikiki** (6 Place de l'Homme de Fer. Tel: 88 75 05 45; open daily) which is diagonally opposite Le Petit Maxim. Up an outdoor stairway you proceed into a bamboo-decorated bar where you find yourself in mixed, but primarily younger company. Many of the people who work in the offices which surround the nearby Place Kléber come over here for an after-hours drink. An excursion into the bar of the **Hotel Sofitel** offers the opportunity to take your aperitif in interesting and somewhat grander surroundings. From the Place Kléber you walk through the Petite Rue de l'Eglise

A bonne choucroute alsacienne !

— five minutes at
the most — to reach this
three-star establishment on the Place
Saint-Pierre-le-Jeune (Tel: 88 32 99 30). In the
bar the journalists of the regional daily newspaper *Dernières
Nouvelles d'Alsace* meet frequently and exchange the latest political
gossip. The clientele also includes business people, delegates to the
European Parliament and well-to-do tourists.

You will know that it is time to dine — around 8pm — when the
amount of traffic in the city centre drops noticeably. The people of
Strasbourg like to dine in restaurants with a homely ambience,
and the restaurants do a thriving trade regardless of the vagaries
of economic cycles. It seems that, no matter how badly things
might be financially, the Strasbourgeoise can always find a few
francs to spend on a good meal. They simply regard eating out as
one of the essentials of life.

An example of a restaurant that satisfies high expectations is
L'Alsace à Table (8 Rue des Francs-Bourgeois. Tel: 88 32 50 62;
open daily; up to 250 francs per person) not far away from the
Place Klèber. Passers-by are attracted by the glass cases displaying
fresh oysters and other sea creatures. In the interior there is a pool
with a splashing fountain from which you can select live lobster.
Among the recommended specialities is the sauerkraut with fresh
salmon, not an obvious choice as a culinary pairing, but surprisingly
delicious nonetheless.

The hearty traditional dishes of the Alsatians, such as sauerkraut
with hot slices of meat and crisply browned sausage, are offered in
outstanding quality (and considerable quantity) in **La Maison des
Tanneurs** (42 Rue du Bain-aux-Plantes. Tel: 88 32 79 70; closed

Sunday and Monday; up to 250 francs per person). This restaurant in the middle of the Petite France section of the old quarter is indeed no secret tip – its quality alone is a powerful advertisement. As a result of its splendid location on the canal, the house also features on countless postcards. Those who reserve their tables promptly will definitely pass a satisfying evening here.

Pleasures for the mind are to be had by visiting the **TNS – Théâtre National de Strasbourg** between eight and ten in the evening. The performances of the TNS are famous far beyond the borders of Alsace. The acting school of the TNS also enjoys a very good reputation nationwide. That must certainly mean something in a country as centralised as France – where cultural and other events always seem to revolve around Paris. Every year the TNS offers a series of noteworthy new presentations. Of course, you must bring with you a very good knowledge of the French language in order to appreciate fully the poetry and the expressive stage language (1 Rue Andre Malraux; Tel: 88 35 63 60).

Sketches, cabaret and regional art are offered in **Choucrouterie**, run by singer and theatre director, Roger Siffer. His intimate theatre – installed in a former sauerkraut factory – is the meeting place for those involved in the regional cultural scene, as is the adjacent restaurant. The mood there is loud and boisterous; sometimes there are even sing-alongs. (20 Rue St Louis, Finkwiller quarter. Tel: 88 36 07 28; closed Monday).

Strasbourg has a lively musical life and offers a broad and varied programme ranging from chamber music concerts and opera to performance of contemporary works. Besides the tradition-filled music festivals, the Strasbourg Philharmonic Orchestra (Orchestre Philharmonic de Strasbourg), under the baton of Austrian director Theodor Guschlbauer, gives regular performances featuring famous soloists. The Rhine Opera (Opera du Rhin, Théâtre Municipal, 19 Place Broglie. Tel: 88 36 43 41) was founded in 1972 by the three cities of Strasbourg, Colmar and Mulhouse as France's first regional opera. As for contemporary music, the Percussions de Strasbourg ensemble has gained a considerable reputation amongst aficionados of modern and experimental forms.

Even after dining and attending the theatre or a concert it is still a little too early for the genuine nightlife of Strasbourg – at least as far as the discos go. At these the mood doesn't quite gel until around midnight. You will find a lot happening on Friday and Saturday; on weekdays the discos are often quiet to dead. In the bars you will already encounter the first night owls gathering around 10pm. To find the right bars in Strasbourg you must have a clear goal. Wandering through the streets and seeing where you wind up does not pay off, since the bars and discotheques are mostly hidden. Let's say for example that you're standing on the Place de la Cathédral scratching your head and wondering what to do. Just walk around the cathedral and along the **Rue des Frères**. This quarter of town belongs to the students. After a few minutes turn right – into the **Rue des Soeurs** – where, on the left-hand side of the street, one of the most popular bars in the city is located – **Les Aviateurs** (12 Rue des Soeurs. Tel: 88 36 52 69; open daily from 6pm–3am). This bar is also popular with singles.

On the opposite side of the same street you can check out the 'Spies' Nest' (**Le Nid d'Espions**, 3 Rue des Soeurs; open daily from 6pm–3am). This bar is small and atmospheric – and the host is always coming up with new ideas for cocktails. From the student quarter it isn't far to the **Krutenau**, a very popular quarter with a series of well-known bars and restaurants. Since the Krutenau (formerly Kräuterau) is located outside of the city centre and has no 'sights', in the classic sense of the word, tourists seldom stray into it. You follow the Rue des Soeurs, which empties into the Rue de l'Abrevoir. From there a little pedestrian bridge leads you over the Ill Canal. Then you follow the Quai des Bateliers from left to right up to the **Rue de Zurich**. This is where the Krutenau quarter begins. Shortly before the Place de Zurich we turn to the left into the narrow Ruelle Sainte Cathérine. The street is not long and during the summer the cars are double-parked here. The points of attraction are **Le Bouchon** (6 Rue Sainte Cathérine; open daily from 7pm–3am) and right next door **Le Festival** (same business hours). These are both 'in' meeting places for the chic; during the summer they spill out onto the

The European Parliament

The astronomical clock in Strasbourg cathedral

street terraces. Behind the lace curtains on the windows of Le Bouchon you will sometimes hear jazz piano music; you can also get a bite to eat here late at night, a *chili con carne*, for example. This nightspot is decorated in a youthful style. The guests are mostly in their later twenties and affluent – the prices are not exactly low. Le Festival next door is similarly upmarket. At the end of the Rue Sainte Cathérine our route continues to the right along the Rue de Zurich up to the **Bar Les Ripoux** (59 Rue de Zurich; open daily from 7pm–3am). Video films are shown here on a big screen.

To get from the Krutenau to a discotheque it is best to take a taxi and have yourself driven to the **Centre Halles** shopping centre. The fashionable meeting place here is **Le Charlie's** (24 Place des Halles; open daily from 10pm–5am). Here the champagne flows freely, and this disco has style. Across the way you go down a staircase into the **Blue Hawaii** (19 Rue du Marais Vert; closed Monday, open from 10pm until dawn) where, despite the name, African ambience prevails – both in the music and in the crowd.

The largest disco in eastern France is located some 5km (3 miles) outside of the city in a northerly direction, about half-way to the village of La Wantzenau. **Le Châlet** (375 Route de la Wantzenau; closed Sunday and Monday; open until 3am; admission 75 francs) is actually more of an entertainment centre with two discotheques (waltzes for the older crowd, pop and rock for the younger), a restaurant, pizzeria, café and dining hall. However, you won't get in wearing jeans and training shoes. The clientele here tends to be very young. A good time to meet people is the 'Encounter Evening' on Tuesday, when at midnight a basket full of womens' shoes is passed around. It's up to the men to figure out who the owners might be.

Just before the Châlet on the right-hand side of the road is **Le Bamboo** (366 Route de la Wantzenau; open Thursday, Friday and Saturday from 10pm–6am), a disco with tropical decor featuring reggae and salsa music. In this pleasure oasis there are regular live music performances.

56

TOUR 6

Tipsy Moments Around Mont Ste-Odile

On the Alsatian Route du Vin from Sélestat to Strasbourg.

Our route today revolves around the protective patroness of Alsace, the Abbess Odile. She took her refuge on **Mount Odilia** – a remarkable, and consequently much-visited, observation point above the Route du Vin in central Alsace. As the starting point for today's journey you can equally well come from Strasbourg, Colmar or Sélestat. The following itenerary starts in **Sélestat**, once Schlettstadt – the famous high temple of humanist philosophy.

Sélestat's **Humanist Library** in the Kornhalle is a year-round destination for people interested in history. In its glass cases you can admire bibliophilic treasures (such as the *Liber Miraculorum Sanctae Fidis*) which were gathered – along with many hundreds of additional handwritten manuscripts and books of engravings –

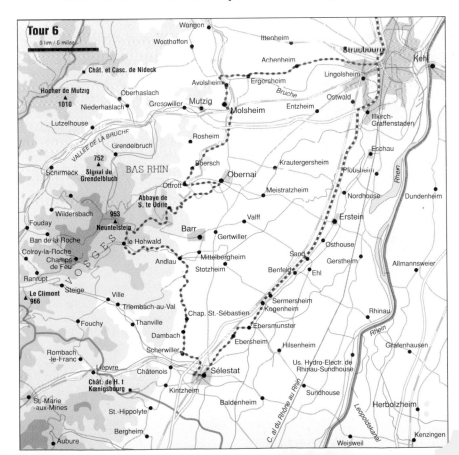

Sélestat

by Beatus Rhenanus and other humanists in the 16th and 17th centuries. On the second Sunday in August the attractive little country town of Sélestat is the destination of some 10,000 visitors. They come in anticipation of the famed **Corso Fleuri** (Flower Parade) which is outstanding among processions of its kind.

We depart the town in the direction of St Dié, then turn off half-right towards Scherwiller and arrive in the **foothill zone**, through which the Route du Vin winds. The half-timbered houses of Dambach, backed by green hills covered with vineyards, are our first foretaste of the landscape as well as culinary pleasures of the 'Wine Route'. **Vente et Degustation** is our guiding motto of the day. Alsatian vintners know what warms the hearts of tourists, and so along the Route du Vin you will see signs directing you to their romantically appointed cellars and sampling rooms. Here you have an overwhelming choice – but, of course, since the quality is so excellent you can confidently stop at any of the vintners, or their associations. Somebody is going to have to miss out on pleasures of the *flûtes*, however; it is best if the driver of your party abstains from sampling, or tastes but does not swallow the wine.

One look at **Itterswiller's** geranium-and-half-timbered splendour will give you cause for rapture – just as will the local gastronomy (at, for example, the **Hotel Arnold** and **Restaurant à l'Aigle**). Shortly past this well-scrubbed vintners' hamlet we turn right in the direction of **Andlau**, which is surrounded by vineyards and the first forests of the Vosges. Art lovers will head for the **monastery** to stare in fascination at the fabulous creatures on the figured frieze high above them on the Romanesque west façade. In the relief on the main portal, towards the left, there is a very graphic, but naive, portrayal of how Eve came to being from Adam's rib: this medieval artist made it clear that women owed their existence to men. As a fitting counterbalance you can discuss emancipation in the **Boeuf Rouge** or in another of Andlau's several restaurants.

Departing from this pretty little village, with its picturesque interior courtyards, we drive uphill through mixed woodlands on our way to Le Hohwald. The **Ferme Relais du Sorbier** is a good place to combine a break with some playtime for the children and perhaps an excursion on horseback. The speciality of the house is *Gratin au Munster*. The health resort **Le Hohwald** is located on a high plateau and the refreshing climate is not the least of its attractions. Here our route branches left to **Mont Ste-Odile**. The road winds through the forests at an altitude of 700m (2,300ft) and provides many good views eastwards over the plain of the Rhine before we come under the mountain's influence.

Mont Ste-Odile is enwrapped in legends and laden with history. Adjacent to the parking area is the Heathen Wall (Mur Païen) a refuge conjectured to have been erected by the Celts. Originally this wall, which is constructed of tremendous stones, was over 10km (6 miles) long; a colossal ring which – despite destruction and decay – still conveys a sense of its titanic proportions in places. Odile, the patron saint of Alsace, is definitely among the most popular personalities between the Rhine and the Vosges; this is obvious from the packed parking area in front of the entrance to the monastery. This 'Daughter of Light' – who founded a monastery on this exposed mountain in the 7th century and is said to have performed many miracles – is portrayed by an oversized statue on the observation terrace. The spot where Odile extended her hands in benediction over Alsace has become a pilgrimage destination, a national sanctuary and place for family outings. Since sanctity and a great view are combined here, as nowhere else in Alsace, the selling of kitsch and religious art flourishes correspondingly.

Because of the crowd it is not likely that you will want to spend much time in this holy place. At the end of the car park a little street branches off half-left towards St Nabor, taking us on a winding route downhill through the woodlands. At the intersection we go left to **Ottrott**, whose cobbled street leads us to several pleasant restaurants (**Hostellerie des Château, Winstub Ami Fritz, Beau Site**), which also specialise in Ottrott's famous red wine. Located 4km (2.5 miles) further on in the forested solitude of the Klingenthal are the Ottrotter castles – a good destination for a hike of about four hours.

Hospitality in Ottrott

We will next make another rewarding side-trip off the Route du Vin with a visit to **Obernai**, one of the most picturesque towns in the whole province. If you look around the marketplace and mentally erase the tourists, advertising signs and cars it is easy to feel yourself transported back to another age – the historical backdrop has somehow remained unharmed. Fitting this frame are the *flammenkuechen* (or *tarte flambée*) and the *hasenpfeffer* prepared from wild rabbit in the **Resturarant La Halle** on the marketplace.

Back to the Wine Route. We need ten minutes to get to **Boersch**. There we can admire one of the most beautiful Renaissance fountains in Alsace along with the city hall, churches and vintners' courtyards. In the **Restaurant aux Pieds de Boeuf** they serve – as everywhere along the Wine Route – an excellent *tarte flambée*, an Alsatian variant of pizza which melts in your mouth. While Boersch still has a feel of rural town, **Rosheim** is rather busier. The Romanesque basilica with its fantastic figures has left its stamp on the symmetrical gables of Rosheim's centre; on the second Sunday in September people stream to the *Corso Fleurie* procession.

The express highway takes us quickly to **Molsheim**. This is a country town whose historic centre can be interpreted as an expression of the Alsatian way of life carved in stone. The Jesuit church is a curious anachronism, built in Gothic style in an age when baroque was the fashion. The market place, with its fountain and Renaissance Metzig (or Butchers' Guild building) forms an attractive focal point to the town. In place of the usual calm, a 'wild west' atmosphere prevails in late June: 'High Noon' takes place before the imposing façades of this historic town (once named Metzig) when Cowboy and Indian Clubs from the area take to the warpath and smoke a peace-pipe along with a glass of Riesling.

In **Avolsheim**, with its little chapel located in an open field, we reach the northernmost tip of the Alsatian Route du Vin. Here the D45 branches off to the right towards Wolxheim and Breuschwickersheim, where the suburbs of Strasbourg are already within reach.

Restaurants

Sélestat

JEAN-FRÉDÉRIC EDEL
7 Rue des Serruriers.
Tel: 88 92 86 55.
Closed Tuesday evening, Wednesday and Sunday evening.
Jean-Fred, as the chef of the house is generally called, has woken Sélestat out of its long culinary slumber. His menu is oriented toward seasonal fresh produce. Complete menus from around £20–45.

AUBERGE DES ALLIÉS
39 Rue des Chevaliers.
Tel: 88 92 09 34.
Here Alsatian specialities, such as the sauerkraut plate, as well as some fine fish, are served at reasonable prices. Complete menus are offered at between £10–20. If you like a romantic atmosphere you will be more than pleased with this rustic wine-tavern.

Le Hohwald:

AUBERGE DU WELSCHBRUCH
North of Le Hohwald toward Neuntelstein.
Tel: 88 08 30 01.
Closed Tuesday during summer, Wednesday afternoon in winter. A picture-book forester's house with a cosy bar. Hearty dishes which will give new strength to forest workers, hikers and skiers. The terrace on the edge of the woods is a peaceful and relaxing place to dine in warm weather.

FERME-AUBERGE LINDENHOF
On the south exit from Le Hohwald next to the youth hostel.
Tel: 88 08 31 98.
Without a reservation you will not get a table in this mountain guest house, since the culinary artistry of chef André Deissler has made his *ferme* famous throughout the region. Munster cheeses are also sold for takeaway, as is true of almost all the Alsatian *ferme-auberges*.

Renaissance Butcher's Guild building in Molsheim

Ottrott

BEAU SITE
1 Rue Général de Gaulle.
Tel: 88 95 80 61.
This restaurant has two dining rooms: the modern *Quatre Saison* serves Alsatian dishes; the rustic *Salle Spindler* is where the gourmets show up. One speciality is the gourmet *Menu Ottrottois* for £40 consisting entirely of products from Ottrott. Try it if you are feeling expansive; some may think it not exactly worth the price!

Andlau

L'AMI FRITZ
8 Rue du Vignoble.
Tel: 88 95 80 81.
Closed Wednesday.
A typical wine tavern with a homely atmosphere. Especially tasty here are the Alsatian specialities such as onion cake and *salat ganseliesl*. Fine French cuisine is offered in complete menus whose prices range between £15–35.

AU BOEUF ROUGE
6 Rue du Docteur Stolz.
Tel: 88 92 96 26.
Closed Wednesday evening and Thursday.
Gourmets prize this restaurant because of its ambience, the friendly reception and – the main reason – for its extensive menus offering a broad variety of cuisine. The desserts are outstanding and the hand-painted wine list is unusually comprehensive even for the Alsace. Complete menus for £15–25.

Hotels

Mont Ste-Odile

HOSTELLERIE DES ODILIENBERGES
Tel: 88 95 80 65.
Lodge right next to the patron saint of Alsace at the summit of Mt Ste-Odile. Rooms are inexpensive and very popular, and as a result are only available by telephone reservation, which must also be confirmed in writing. Rooms cost £8–25.

Obernai

LE PARC
169 Rue du Général Gourand.
Tel: 88 95 50 08.
This comfortable hotel also has a restaurant serving gourmet cuisine whose menu ranges from lamb to snails and langoustines. The complete gourmet menu costs £35. Room prices cover a range from £35–60.

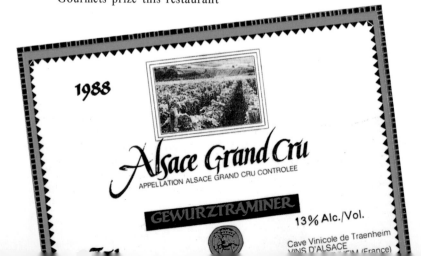

Haut-Koenigsbourg Château

Children, as well as adults, will love the picture-book castle of Haut-Koenigsbourg. Make sure that you reserve at least a week in advance for the more sophisticated gourmet delights of L'Auberge de L'Ill restaurant.

Leaving Sélestat, follow the signs to Kintzheim. Soon you will see a Ferris wheel, the unmistakable sign of an **amusement park** which – for those of us with children – is almost impossible to drive past. This amusement park is redolent of the 1950s and doesn't – by a long shot – have as many attractions as more

Kintzheim

modern versions. Even so, at the *Parc d'animaux* you can spend an entertaining hour or so looking at the horses, storks, aquariums and a King Kong with eyes that simply radiate terror.

In Kintzheim there are several signs pointing the way to the Haut-Koenigsbourg (*burg* is German for castle). The road goes uphill and, after several hundred metres, a minor road branches off left to the **Volerie des Aigles** – the Eagles' Preserve. This is housed in the Château de Kintzheim. If you want to watch a spectacular presentation of the flight of condors, vultures and golden eagles from really close up, then you will take a seat in the front row in the middle of the medieval castle's courtyard. These tremendous birds climb high and then plummet faster than arrows, skimming close over the heads of the onlookers. Under clear skies these kings of the heavens demonstrate their art of flying on weekdays at 3pm and 4pm; weekends at 2.30pm and 5pm. Tel: 88 92 84 33; admission 30 francs for adults; 15 francs for children.

A few kilometres further up towards the mountains you will find the **Montagne des Singes** (Mountain of the Apes), located off to the right of the approach road to the Haut-Koenigsbourg. This is

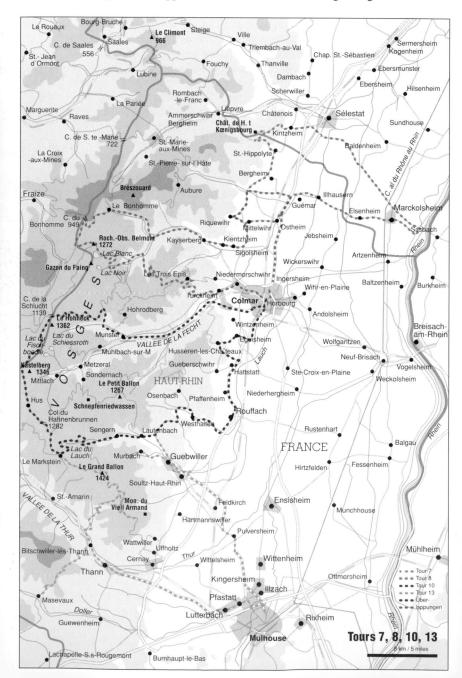

an experience that is just made for children to share with their parents. A circular path leads you through the forest of the Vosges, in which several hundred Barbary apes from the Atlas Mountains in North Africa have their new home. At the entrance gate each visitor receives a handful of popcorn to feed our next closest evolutionary relatives. When a mother ape approaches with her offspring on her back, the cameras start to click and visitors can hardly get their fill of the moving scene. Next door an experienced patriarch with a bored look on his face reaches for the popcorn offered him – and then, quick as lightning, whips around and pummels a rival into retreat. April–October the mountain is open from 10am–noon and 2pm–6pm. Tel: 88 92 11 09; admission costs 15 francs for adults; 10 francs for children.

What – from a distance – looks more like a pencil stub reveals itself closer up to be one of the most impressive of all the Alsatian castles: Haut-Koenigsbourg presents a backdrop straight out of a medieval picture-book, even though it is not yet a hundred years old. The original castle dates from the 12th century and was left a ruin after the Thirty Years' War. The castle ruins were later presented to the Prussian Kaiser Wilhelm II who restored it as a symbol of German involvement in Alsace. Rebuilding work began in 1899 with no attempt at historical authenticity but more as an idealised image of what a medieval castle may have looked like.

Today it draws visitors from near and far. Touring the rooms

Haut-Koenigsbourg

and halls with their 'authentic' period furnishings, ascending the tower to the bastions you will feel yourself transported back to a valiant knight's castle of the 15th century. The view over the three-stage enclosure walls, over towers and graves and on down to the Rhine Valley, is magnificent and the commanding location of the Haut-Koenigsbourg is impossible to overlook. Since nowadays more and more people take pleasure in visiting historic monuments and practically storm the stony testimonies to the past, this Wilhelminian magic castle is besieged by thousands of visitors on weekends. It is therefore recommended that you undertake your personal conquest of the castle on one of the quieter days. This prime Alsatian attraction can be seen daily from 9am–noon and

Auberge de l'Ill

1–6pm; admission is 22 francs for adults and 12 francs for children.

For the drive back to the Rhine river-plain we recommend the **St Hippolyte** route. This pretty little winemakers' village has a good address for gourmets – **Aux Ducs de Lorraine**. This route takes us along the Alsatian Route du Vin again and, considering the abundant serving of flora, fauna and history we've had today you could – with a good conscience – end your excursion over a good meal with wine in St Hippolyte.

If, however, you would like to make your acquaintance with the heraldic symbol of Alsace in the flesh, then you can take yet another outing on the wine route up to **Hunawihr**. This village lies between the 'tourism pearls' of Ribeauvillé and Riquewihr; it is embedded in the best Alsatian wine area and located at the entrance to the village is the **Centre de Réintroduction des Cigognes** – the 'Stork Centre'.

The park was established in order to help the almost-extinct Alsatian storks back on their feet – a plan which is succeeding. Storks were once common in Alsace, returning here every summer after wintering in Central Africa. Hunting and the use of agricultural pesticides severely reduced their numbers. The Stork Centre began by importing young birds from Africa in the late 1960s. Today, besides the other animal species in the Hunawihr stork preserve you can scrutinize some 150 long-billed storks which stay in the Alsace year-round – they are no longer migratory birds. A pond in the park further presents you with the opportunity – at 3, 4 and 5pm – to watch cormorants and penguins catch fish at lightning speed.

The Centre des Cigognes is open between April and October from 10am–noon and 2–6pm. Admission: adults 25 francs and children 15 francs. On the other side of the parking area is yet another attraction: an enchanting glass dome filled with exotic butterflies. You can imagine yourself – surrounded by the colourful and magnificent *papillon* – in some kind of stylised primeval forest.

The return drive from Hunawihr back to the Rhine passes through Ostheim, Guémar and Illhausern. The flat, monotonous Rhine river-plain conceals – in the last place you would expect it *the* Alsatian gourmet temple par excellence: the **Auberge de l'Ill** of the Haeberlin brothers. Spontaneous visits are pointless: there is no way you will get a table without booking at least a week in advance in this world-famous high temple of the culinary arts. Songs in praise of the Haeberlins are legion, and the mouth of any gourmet will begin to water at the thought of the restaurant's regional dishes – brought to the highest state of perfection: *baeckeoffe* with truffles, partridge with green wheat, rabbit salad – with which a *Crémant d'Alsace*, taken on the auberge's terrace under the trees of the Ill riverbank, harmonises most wonderfully.

Restaurants

Kintzheim

CHAVEAU BRUNSTEIN
Tel: 88 82 04 81.
Closed Monday.
The *flammenkuchen* (or *tarte flambée*) served on weekends from 4pm on the terrace tastes especially good.

AUBERGE SAINT-MARTIN
80 Rue de la Liberté.
Tel: 88 82 04 78.
Closed Wednesday as well as Thursday lunch.
An Alsatian family business always full of guests who come to sample the outstanding *baeckeoffe* and potatoes au gratin with goose liver. The weekend speciality of this good, typical and authentic auberge is the *tarte flambée*.

Ribeauvillé:

ZUM PFIFFERHUS
14 Grand'Rue.
Tel: 89 73 62 28.
Closed Wednesday and Thursday.
This former Guildhouse of the Pfifferdai has a picture-book façade. The cuisine is solidly regional and the prices are reasonable consequently there is a great crush for seating during the high season.

Children's park near Kintzheim

DES VOSGES
2 Grand'Rue.
Tel: 89 73 61 39.
Closed Monday and Tuesday.
A gourmet restaurant with a long-established reputation. Maître Joseph Matter prepares fish specialities and wild game dishes of the very first quality. Complete menus range from £20–£40.

Guémar

FERME HODLER
Between Ribeauvillé and Guemar; look for the entrance signs.
Tel: 89 73 62 32.
At this large dairy farm you can buy the home-produced Munster cheese, creamy *fromage blanc* and excellent youghurt.

Illhausern

AUBERGE DE L'ILL
Rue de Collonges.
Tel: 89 71 83 23.
Closed Monday and Tuesday.
This pearl of Alsatian – and, indeed of French – culinary arts is virtually beyond description. The praises of the three Haeberlins (Jean-Pierre, Paul and Marc) are so often sung – in the highest tones – that without reservations made well in advance there isn't *any chance at all* of getting a seat in this elegant restaurant.

Like no other in the Alsace, this gourmet's house of worship is a culinary institution – but the devoted gourmets who come here must have well-padded wallets or gold-plated credit cards.

The secret of Chefs Paul and Marc is to prepare traditional Alsatian dishes with creative refinement and using produce of the highest quality so as to bring their offerings to the pinnacle of flavour. The Haeberlins have made Illhausern – a quiet little country town on the banks of the Ill river – the most famous village in the Alsace.

The Auberge sits by the riverside in a beautiful setting, best appreciated if you go there for lunch and begin with an aperitif on the terrace. The prices might seem exaggerated to the cost-conscious: complete menus range between £45 and £80; *à la carte* offerings start at £80. It goes without saying that the Haeberlins employ a world champion among oenologists – Serge Dubs rules over 75,000 bottles of the finest character.

Artzenheim

AUBERGE D'ARTZENHEIM
30 Rue du Sponeck.
Tel: 89 71 60 51.
Closed Monday evening and Tuesday.
In Marckolsheim head in the direction of Neuf Brisach and you will wind up in the sleepy little village of Artzenheim, which conceals a culinary secret: among Alsatians this Auberge has enjoyed a good reputation for many years because of its fish and meat dishes which are of the best quality at moderate prices. The ambience of the restaurant's various dining areas makes the experience even more of a pleasure.

Imperial Cities, Vineyards and Observation Points

From Colmar to the Lac Blanc and the Route du Vin.
Colmar is a good place to start to appreciate the contrast between the gentle lands along the Route du Vin and the rather more dramatic Central Vosges. From Colmar, depart the city in the direction of Türkheim. As is so often true in France the medieval core of Colmar is concealed by a shell of hideous bunker-like apartment blocks, factories, gas stations and supermarkets. Pass New Colmar on the arterial road towards the west and reach Route Nationale 83. Turn off to the right towards **Türkheim** and, just before the tremendous city gate, find a parking place.

According to an Alsatian proverb this area is supposed to grow the best wine in the land. Here in the idyllic alleys of this medieval vintners' town you will find both tasting rooms and the right place to buy. Those with style drink their Alsatian wines from a *verre taillée* – a shimmering dark-green glass with a slender neck which balances nicely in the hand. In the **Cellier** of Jean Huck (on the main street) six unengraved glasses cost as little as 50 francs. Compare this with the high prices in Strasbourg, Colmar or Riquewihr! Just a few strides away from the Cellier is the **Codec Supermarket** where you can purchase the wine specialities of Türkheim at the same prices as in the **Cave Vinicole**, located at the village exit in the direction of Münster. Naturally, in the cellers the prices are a good bit higher.

Gradually we begin to detect the mood of the Vosges. The road towards Trois Epis winds its way gently into the heights; the air becomes fresher – much more pleasant than the humid atmosphere of the Rhine river-plain, especially in summer. Mixed woodlands now take the place of vineyards. After several hairpin bends we arrive in **Trois Epis**, a *Station Climatique* – in other words a health resort. Here there are hotels and restaurants *en masse*, since Trois Epis is very popular among the Alsatians as a holiday resort with good, fresh air. Past the high **Plateau of Labaroche** (beautiful hiking trails), we glimpse the green **Valley of Orbey**; here slate, instead of half-timbered construction, is prevalent. On reaching the main road, turn left in the direction of Les Lacs and the Col de Bonhomme.

Shortly before Lac Blanc, on the right-hand side, a little road branches off to the **Ferme-Auberge du Pré-Bracot**. There you can sample their simple, but delicious, mountain-farmer dishes; for example, an outstanding *tourte* (meat pastry) or a *baeckeoffe* (only on ordering ahead; Tel: 89 71 25 29). The children can also pick berries here from the broad meadows or show off their bravery on the steep slippery slide. It is a short step to the **Lac Noir** (fork to the left) and the **Lac Blanc**. These two Vosges lakes are only suitable for swimming for those with very tough constitutions; however, you can take a pleasant walk along their stony shores, buy some mountain honey (60 francs) or set out on a longer hike through the mountains.

The **Col de Bonhomme** – the 'high-point' of this tour – is along the ridge-top road called the *Route des Crètes*. We turn off towards Colmar at the intersection; a good road winds its way steadily downhill through coniferous forests and passes **Lapoutrole** with its hiking paths, its wine museum, ski-lifts and cross-country ski trails. Those who are fans of Albert Schweitzer will know of **Kaysersberg**. The legendary doctor of the primeval African forests and winner of the Nobel Peace Prize enjoys a much higher degree of recognition in Germany than in France, thus German is clearly dominant in the house of his birth, which is outfitted as a memorial to him. From here you can park the car and walk the few steps to the White Bridge which sums up the romance and valiant bearing of Alsace. In order to deepen this impression, immerse yourself in the little alleyways beyond the main street, which is overloaded with tourists!

In Riquewihr

A typical wine-route village

It would be quite understandable if you decided, in view of the half-timbered façades in Kaysersberg, to end your tour here, passing by Kientzheim castle and Sigolsheim, driving on to the N83 and then heading back south to Colmar. However, if you want to experience an atmosphere exceeding even that of Kaysersberg, then set your sights northward on the N83: **Riquewihr** is located only 7km (5 miles) distant, and prides itself as being nothing less than the most beautiful village in France.

Superlatives – also with reference to the crowds and the tasteless excesses of tourism – have become Riquewihr's trademarks. Admittedly, the crowds are there for a reason – the appearance of the town, which looks as if it was cast in a medieval mould. Happily, all of Riquewihr has been declared a pedestrian zone – on the other side of the city walls the parking lots full of cars form a second ring around the town. This picturesque winemakers' town has places for the contemplation of history at both its east and west ends: 'below' is a **Postal Museum** (open daily except Tuesday 10am–noon and 2–6pm); 'above' is the **Doldermuseum** (open daily 10am–noon and 2–6pm; afternoons only at weekends). Housed in an imposing guard tower, the Doldermuseum forms a fitting final flourish to Riquewihr, surrounded on all sides by famed vineyards.

It is all but impossible to give special restaurant tips in this 'El Dorado' of tourism. The abundance of choices is gigantic and ranges from fast food up to *choucroute garnie* and nouvelle cuisine. But beware: prices

Pfifferdai (Piper's) Festival in Ribeauvillé

are, for the most part, even more exorbitant than in the other wine villages – the tourist must pay tribute. The organisers of this Alsatian 'open-air stage' have also provided all the accessories needed to convey a 'genuine' sense of life here. Of course, it goes without saying that geraniums decorate the half-timbered houses, and a girl in traditional costume sits patiently at the fountain as the masses of visitors keep their cameras whirring without pause.

Those who have had their fill of the sights here and seek yet more specialities can drive further north on the N83 and turn left toward **Hunawihr**. There, in the **Centre de Réintroduction des Cigognes**, a number of vivacious storks – as opposed to the plastic variety to be had all over Riquewihr – await your visit (see page 66 for further details; open April–October; 10am–noon and 2–6pm. Admission 25 francs for adults and 15 francs for children).

The next stage of our journey along this route – so larded with interesting villages – is **Ribeauvillé**. Here too, the storming crowds stay within reasonable limits only on weekdays and outside of the high season, since the former Rappoltsweiler also boasts an excess of romantic Alsatian half-timbered architecture.

Park your car outside the core of the town and stroll up the gently ascending **Grand'Rue** through the **Metzgerturm Gate** (Butcher's Tower). To your right and left are half-timbered buildings, crimson floral decorations, the colourfully tiled church roof and direction signs to vintners and restaurants.

A gigantic crush prevails on *Pfifferdai*, which takes place on the first Sunday in September, when this pretty little town is full of music and groups in traditional costume – living expression of the 'Piper Kingdom' which the lord of Rappoltstein proclaimed in the Middle Ages. The **Pfifferhus** (No 14 on the main street) was at that time the guildhall of the musicians who secured their existence here in Ribeauvillé. Today it is a restaurant serving reasonably priced regional cuisine.

When you have had your fill of Ribeauvillé you could, if you were really feeling energetic, walk up to the well-preserved remains of Ulrichsburg castle nearby. Most of us, though, will be content to drive via the N83 back to Colmar in anticipation of an evening over good food and wine.

Restaurants

Türkheim

CAVEAU LE CHEMIN DE RONDE
Porte de Munster.
Tel: 89 27 38 27.
Closed Tuesday.
For a change, here we have a restaurant distinguished for a dish that is not all that common in Alsace despite the proximity of Switzerland: fondue in wine sauce.

L'HOMME SAUVAGE
19 Grand'Rue.
Tel: 89 27 32 11.
Closed Monday evening and Wednesday.
Marc Decker, the young chef here, is considered an up-and-coming talent; his restaurant is a noteworthy stop on any culinary tour of the Alsace. Decker's fine fish dishes delight the palate just as well as the excellently prepared regional speciality – chicken pieces in Riesling wine. Prices are reasonable with complete menus available in the region of £15–35.

Niedermorschwihr

CAVEAU MORAKOPF
7 Rue des Trois Epis.
Tel: 89 27 05 10.
Closed Sunday.
A warm, pleasant and genuine wine-tavern with hearty Alsatian cuisine at good prices. As a result expect a gigantic crowd – without reservations you can (almost) forget it. A la carte from as little as £12.

Lac Blanc

FERME-AUBERGE DU PRÉ-BRACOT
Between the town of Orbey and the Lac Blanc.
Tel: 89 71 25 29.
Closed Monday.
This *ferme* on the edge of a high valley in the Vosges serves mountain-farmer dishes – in the high altitude the *baeckeoffe*, *tourte* and mushroom dishes taste especially good.

Kaysersberg

LE CHAMBARD
9 Rue du Général de Gaulle.
Tel: 89 47 10 17.
Closed Monday and Tuesday lunchtimes.

Visitor to the Hunawihr stork centre

Guests can choose between the cosy tavern and the elegant salon in order to experience some of the best of Alsatian gastronomy, in the town of Albert Schweitzer's birth. Goose liver paté, fish with marvellously composed sauces, dessert orgies: gourmets, what more can you ask for? The complete connoisseur menu costs just over £25, whereas dishes chosen from the à la carte menu will cost you up to £50.

Riquewihr

L'ECURIE
15 Rue du Général de Gaulle.
Tel: 89 47 92 48.
Closed Sunday evening and all day Monday.
L'Ecurie has successfully managed to provide unstinting quality in this tourist's romping-ground where most seem content with the run-of-the-mill. The wine-tavern, reached through a paved courtyard, is especially appealing. The complete menus here cost around £10–12. In the neighbouring restaurant by the same name the prices and the quality are higher.

AUBERGE DU SCHOENENBOURG
2 Rue de la Piscine.
Tel: 89 47 92 28.
Closed Wednesday evening and Thursday.
Proprietor François Kiener, a pupil of the Haeberlins, cares as few others do for the culinary reputation of Riquewihr, which is otherwise starting to be dominated by fast food. Naturally, the delicious food here costs a bit more than assembly-line sauerkraut. The house speciality is langoustines with noodles – consumed with a locally produced Tokay d'Alsace. Complete menus: £25–40.

Hotel

Trois Epis

LE HOHLANDSBOURG
Place de l'Eglise.
Tel: 89 49 80 65.
This famous grand hotel is located at a refreshingly high altitude and the fact that it is one of the best hotels in Alsace is reflected in the prices: rooms cost £80–£110; suites £120–220. Four stars (and the pleasures of luxury accomodation) also have their price in Alsace. In the Auberge, however, you can dine heartily. The menu prices are a moderate £9–20.

Colmar's Pearls

Art treasures and half-timbered idyll – a pilgrimage destination for art fans of the world.

This upper-Alsatian capital city owes its fame above all to the gifted Matthias Grünewald. His **Isenheim Altar** painted in 1512 is the showpiece of the **Unterlinden Museum**. Grünewald's visionary masterpiece imbued with the messages of Christian belief, is one the great works of late medieval art. Thus tourist-pilgrims flock to the Unterlinden Museum to stare in fascination at these fantastic portrayals of biblical themes. Despite the massive crowd this mural-altar still leaves an overwhelming impression. We can imagine how the gentle Virgin, the dramatic Crucifixion and the unearthly radiance of the Resurrection must have affected Grünewald's contemporaries. With reverentially lowered voices, guides point out details, directing the eyes of visitors towards the over-large finger of Antonious, or the choir of angels and its be-horned Lucifer.

After the Louvre in Paris, the Unterlinden Museum registers the biggest crowds in France. If you want to contemplate Grünewald's masterpiece close up, then avoid Sunday in the holiday season. The best overall view of the altar panels can be had from the choir

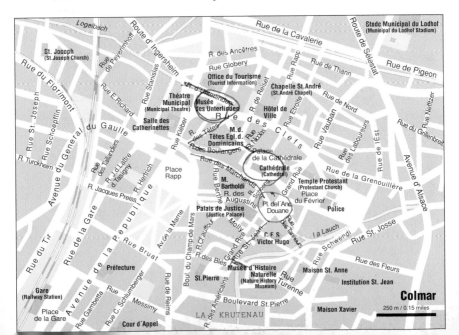

The 'Virgin of the Rose-Bush', Dominican Church

gallery in the Colmar cloister chapel (reached through a side entrance to the cloister). If you climb up the stairs here you will soon discover that the Unterlinden Museum shelters many more art treasures and upper-Rhine handicrafts (including toys). Give yourself plenty of time for the tour.

The Unterlinden Museum is an ideal starting point for our tour through Colmar, not least because there is an easily accessible parking area very close by. From there we stroll past the *Office de Tourisme* onto the **Place d'Unterlinden**. The half-timbered buildings, shopping alleys, street cafés and fountains around the museum already provide a taste of Colmar's specialities. We turn into the **Rue des Têtes** (Street of Heads). On the left-hand side of the street you cannot miss the Renaissance façade ornamented with 100 stone faces – the **Maison des Têtes** (Tel: 89 24 43 43; closed Sunday and Monday). Hiding behind the entrance is a good wine-tavern. The idyllic interior courtyard is a good spot for a rest.

Colmar's **pedestrian zone** starts with the **Rue des Boulanges** (to the left, off the Rue des Têtes). It is without doubt a garden of paradise for tourists, full of art, culture – and kitsch. When the narrow alley of half-timbered houses broadens into the **Place des Dominicans**, the next highpoint is before you. The 'Virgin of the Rose-Bush', painted in 1473 by Martin Schongauer, graces the choir of the **Dominican Church**, and the face of the Virgin, seated within a symbolic rose garden, is a sight which none who has seen it is ever likely to forget. The church it-

Riverside walk, Colmar

self is a fine late 13th-century building with 14th-century stained glass depicting scenes from the New Testament.

From the Eglise des Dominicains to the colourfully roofed St Martin's Cathedral we get a good look at the standard fare of Colmar: *flûtes* and storks, *pâtisseries*, cafés and snack-booths. Apart from the glazed tiles of its roof, St Martin's looks plain at first sight. Close inspection reveals a superb portal to the southern transept carved with scenes from the Last Judgement. The interior suffered during the French Revolution when it was turned into a 'Temple of Reason', although some 14th-century glass remains.

Did you know that we have a sculptor from Colmar to thank for New York's Statue of Liberty? His name is August Bartholdi, and his work *en miniature* can be examined in his museum on the **Rue des Marchands**. From here its only a few steps to the **Maison Pfister**, on the south side of the cathedral square. With its painted wooden balconies and the little bay-windowed tower the Maison Pfister is the quintessence of Old Colmar and one of the most popular photo-motifs in town. Just opposite is a gold-mine for

Colmar

collectors of old books: 'Read and Snoop' is this shop's translated name (*Lire et Chiner*), located in the Eglingsdoerfer-Schwarz house. You don't have to pay a fortune here for old postcards and books. While picking them out you can look forward to a glass of wine in the neighbouring **Luxhof**.

The visiting throngs, including ourselves, now have the **Ancienne Douane** (Old Customs House) as our destination. All we have to do is follow the postcard stands to come upon the Place de l'Ancienne Douane. This is surrounded by half-timbered architecture, and its eastern side is formed by the glazed-tiled old Customs House. Climb the staircase to the upper-floor exhibition area and turn around: a gasp of wonder at the idyllic scene is certain.

If you are hungry and thirsty from your tour there is an overwhelming selection of cafés around the Place de l'Ancienne Douane. The **Winstub** behind the Customs House in Rue des Tanneurs has an attractive, shady garden. The **Quartier des Tanneurs** (Tanner's Quarter) is a picturesque frame for our continued exploration of the city. We follow the **Rue St Jean** in a southwesterly direction and then turn left to the bridge over the **Lauch**. You will find the view of half-timbered houses overflowing with geraniums and staggered gables along the riverbank either enchantingly beautiful, or artificially arranged, decide for yourself. At any rate Petite Venice is firmly in the hands of the international visitors – and the banks of the Lauch form one of Colmar's better sides.

Colmar's old quarter

The **Winstub de Krutenau** provides not only an observation platform, it is also a port of call for boat-parties on the Lauch. Only a few strides further on, located beneath the bridge which carries the Boulevard St Pierre over the Lauch, we can gaze at the scene from the terrace of **Caveau St Pierre**, only occasionally disrupted by the tourists who walk past our table.

We have reached the turning point of our walk through town; next we turn to the northeast, on the right bank of the Lauch, passing by the Museum of Natural History. Here the houses shelter fish restaurants; for example, **Aux Trois Poissons**. In the *poissonerie* **Jean B Wertz** you can buy river and lake fish directly; this is understandably popular amongst Colmar residents.

Follow the direction signs to the Quartier des Tanneurs over the Lauch bridge and after a few steps you will arrive again at the historic Ancienne Douane. Let your spirit guide you: if you haven't had enough of this romantic half-timber fantasyland then walk back to the Unterlinden square. If you want to see what shopping Colmar has to offer, turn right onto the Grand'Rue and go to the Place de la Cathédrale. From there the Unterlinden Museum and the parking area are only a short distance to the north.

Restaurants

LE FER ROUGE
52 Grand'Rue.
Tel: 89 41 37 24.
Closed Sunday evening and all day Monday.
The wild game and fish dishes of this famous restaurant are among the most delicious to be had in Colmar. Complete menus from £25–£50.

CHEZ HANSI
23 Rue des Marchands.
Tel: 89 24 48 55.
Closed Wednesday evening and all day Thursday.
This tavern within view of the Fer Rouge is a bit cosier and more Alsatian. A typical dish would be the sauerkraut plate – the best in Colmar.

S'PARISER STEWWELE
4 Place Jeanne d'Arc.
Tel: 89 41 42 33.
Closed Wednesday.
Despite the Parisian element in the name, this wine-tavern is a Colmar institution. The hearty dishes here, such as Munster cheese or ham with potatoes, go well with the house wines. A good place to sit and chat.

WINSTUB FLORY
1 Rue Mangold.
Tel: 89 41 78 80.
Closed Tuesday evening and all day Wednesday.
In addition to the Alsatian cuisine, *couscous* is a house speciality. On the terrace you can eat Arabic – with Colmar before your eyes.

DA ALBERTO
24 Rue des Marchands.
Tel: 89 23 37 89.
Closed Sunday evening and all day Monday.
Pizzerias generally serve just what the tourist expects who wants to stuff his gullet – and those of his children – in a short time at minimal expense: not exactly *dining*. Don't plan on this at Monsieur Bradi's. He may bear an Italian name, but he has nothing in common with the pizza baker. He is considered to be the 'Noodle Pope' of the Alsace, and his tagliatelli, carpaccio and forest-mushroom risotto will give gourmets a chance to taste the fact that the cradle of France's *nouvelle cuisine* actually stands in Italy.

Hotels

ALTÉA CHAMP DE MARS
Avenue de la Marne.
Tel: 89 41 54 54.
A modern hotel with modern rooms which could be anywhere other than in Alsace. Rooms: £30–40.

LE MARECHAL
4 Place des Six Montagnes Noires.
Tel: 89 41 60 32.
In the heart of Petite Venice and one of the most charming hotels in Colmar. You will also eat well in its restaurant. Room prices correspond to the location: £30–85.

MOTEL AZUR
50 Route de Strasbourg.
Tel: 89 41 32 15.
A suggestion in case finding lodging elsewhere doesn't work out and you are looking for a reasonably priced and attractive motel complete with garden. Rooms: £15–25.

Tour 10

High Pleasures in the High Vosges

The Route des Crêtes from Colmar and back.

Visitors who haven't yet got much beyond the Route de Vin must believe that the Alsace is a rather tame landscape – a mosaic composed of grapes, sauerkraut, half-timbered houses and geraniums. This is far from the truth: on today's journey we will get to know the more dramatic side of Alsace, and we'll see for ourselves that the passes of the High Vosges have an almost alpine character.

The starting point today is Colmar or one of the pretty little winemakers' villages surrounding it. From this 'display-city' of the upper Alsace we hurry past its rather less-attractive suburbs, taking the D417 and following the signs to **Épinal** and **Gérardmer**. The Munster Valley starts just past Wintzenheim; the first section, however, is not worth stopping for. Industry dominates the scene until **Munster**.

The town of Munster itself has a lively tourist trade; a stop in this lively little city is by no means just about cheese, even if this has become its trademark. A ripe Munster with caraway seed – served with finely sliced onions and parsley or even anise and rounded off with fresh farmer's bread and a dry white wine; what more could you want in order to get a real taste of the Vosges? You can, of course, buy Munster cheese in Munster, but it is more fun to pay a visit to a farmer along the **Route du Fromage**, where you can purchase this highly aromatic raw cheese directly from the producer. We will stop by several of these on our tour.

At **Soultzeren** work at the steering wheel really starts to be tough. From there on the route really goes uphill – up-mountain rather – passing by the first of the *téléskis*, which is what ski-lifts are called in French. To the left a path branches off towards the Centre des Vacances **Les Sources**. Stop here if you want to go

horse-riding in idyllic forest solitude (children are catered for here, too). Just before you reach the summit of the ridge, you should park in one of the parking bays which are carved into the rock on the pass road. There is no better view in the whole of the Vosges than the one from the nearby summit, across to rugged mountain cliffs and the rounded peak of the Hohneck, over the heavily forested **Fecht High Valley**. Those who want to go hiking in the most impressive part of these central mountains are in the right place at the **Col de la Schlucht**. Just off to the left is the beginning of the **Sentier des Roches** – the 'Path of Cliffs' – which does every justice to its name. On this most beautiful of Alsatian hiking paths you proceed through a craggy world into the gentle valley of Frankenthal; from there the path takes the strenuous way up to the summit of the Hohneck, from which you hike back into the Col de la Schlucht. This day's hike is only for the physically fit – but the experience of nature more than compensates for the fatigue.

Today we'll take the more comfortable route; after reaching the top of the pass (1,139m/3,737ft) and driving past the Col de la Schlucht tourist centre, we first of all continue straight ahead in the direction of Gérardmer, soon turning left onto the Route des Crêtes. The **Jardin d'Altitude** is a *must* for botany fans – an alpine Garden of Eden with a wealth of plants from the Alps, the Andes, the Himalayas and, naturally, the High Vosges. This garden is maintained by the University of Nancy. Afterwards a minor road full of pot-holes branches off to the left up to the **Hohneck**, whose 1,362m (4,468ft) guarantee a great panorama.

The Route des Crêtes originated from military planning. During World War I the French wanted to prevent their German opponents from being able to observe their troop movements in the Vosges; therefore they laid out a mountain road to the west of the ridgeline. As a result, the route provides expansive views far to the west over the forests of the Vosges, while Germany remains hidden from view; anyone who wants to spy on it will have to get out of the car. Often your efforts will be in vain: the Rhine river-plain and the Black Forest are often enshrouded in mist. As the bird flies the distance from the Hohneck to the Feldberg (the famous German mountain) is just about 100km (62 miles).

On our next leg we have a head-spinning number of choices: towards which *ferme-auberge* should we proceed? To the right and left along the ridge road there is one direction sign after another. In the high season and on Sundays don't even hope for a friendly welcome at a near-empty mountain guest-house: even the *fermes-auberges* set back some distance from the Route des Crêtes are

firmly in the hands of hikers and automobile excursionists. Where you finally settle down is – in the last analysis – a matter of taste. For example, you can avoid the tourist bus-loads if you seek out the **Ferme-Auberge du Kastelberg**; it is reached over a small five-kilometer (three-mile) forest road to our left. The view from there into the mountain panorama is intoxicating, and the Munster cheese tastes especially good during a rest on the wooden benches in front of the farmstead. At the **Ferme-Auberge du Rothenbach** (1km past the Firstmiss, where the path up to the Wildenstein branches off from the Route des Crêtes) the specialities include *baeckeoffe* and pastries with goat's cheese. Nature lovers should seek out this farmstead, since guided hikes are offered which go up into the high moors around the Rothenbachkopf (reservations and information on 89 82 25 39).

At the **Markstein** it's the same in summer or winter – snack booths everywhere. Fast food in the High Vosges? Many skiers and people out for some air no longer pass up this variation of New World nouvelle cuisine. A development which would still have been almost unimaginable a few years ago has won ground even in

France, although gourmets may turn up their noses. The 1,200m (3,937ft) high Markstein has all sorts of other entertainments to quicken the pulse of tourists, including a summer toboggan-run and ski lifts.

After the Markstein we keep to the right at the intersection, heading towards Lautenbach and Guebwiller. The D430 winds its way steeply downhill before **Lautenbach** comes into view. In Buhl the road has a turn-off to the Romanesque Murbach Monastery, a side-excursion which art lovers will consider unmissable, as the harmony and contrast between nature and the works of man has rarely been as pleasing as it is in this quiet valley of the Vosges.

Those who have seen enough can drive from Lautenbach and Murbach to **Guebwiller** (with its interesting church); from there head onto the high-speed motorway which takes you past **Rouffach** (with an extraordinary medieval market-place even for the Alsace!) and back to Colmar. Those with more time can take an easier-going alternative: the drive from Lautenbach through quiet vintners' villages to Eguisheim. Fortunately, this southern portion of the Alsatian Route du Vin doesn't suffer from such an overwhelming flood of tourists as the region between Kaysersberg, Riquewihr and Ribeauvillé – partly because its attractions are not as spectacular. Even so, those who wander through the villages of Soultzmatt, Westhalten, Gueberschwihr or Obermorschwihr with open eyes will discover landscape which has grown naturally – it doesn't look artificial. From Gueberschwihr we proceed to Hattstatt and soon turn off to the left from the motorway to the wine village of Husseren-les-Châteaux. Those who want to can then explore the **Five-Mountain Road** and return to Colmar via the Munster Valley. This, however, would mean missing Eguisheim, an inexcusable mistake during any visit to Alsace.

Eguisheim

No other city in the Upper Rhine has managed to preserve its medieval face as authentically as **Eguisheim**. Portions of the ring-wall around the centre of the town can be seen from **Drei Exen** on the Castle Road, as you approach. Even so, you don't really appreciate the wonderful amalgamation of fortifications and residential houses until you get closer to the town on the circle route, the **Circuit Touristique**. Half-timbered buildings, fountains, romantic interior courtyards and decorative flowers all play their part in the scene. One postcard view of romantic cobbled streets, geranium-hung balconies and jettied upper storeys surpasses the next.

In the **Caveau d'Eguisheim** you can take a glass or two of Riesling and, since this vintners' town produces remarkable wines, you will probably not be able to resist a visit to a *vente directe* (direct-sales outlet).

Restaurants

Munster

LA CIGOGNE
4 Place du Marché.
Tel: 89 77 32 27.
Closed Sunday evening and all day Monday.
The fillet of pike in Riesling is particularly good in this restaurant, which is situated across from the city hall; Alsatian specialities, such as *spaetzle* and sauerkraut, also appear on the menu. Medium prices.

Hohneck

FERME-AUBERGE DU KASTELBERG
On the Route des Crêtes by the Ferme-Auberge Breitzousen; take the road, signposted to the Ferme-Auberge, branch off to the left toward the Kastelberg; the farmstead is located 5km (3 miles) down the road.
Tel: 89 77 62 25.
Open from mid-May to October. The Hohneck is a hikers paradise. Afterwards a hearty omelette in the Ferme is an excellent restorative.

FERME-AUBERGE DU ROTHENBACH
On the Route des Crêtes. 1km past the Firstmiss, turn off to the right to the Wildenstein. The Ferme is within view of the Route des Crêtes.
Tel: 89 82 25 39.
Open from mid-May to October. Specialities include *baeckeoffe*, cheeses and guided nature tours (the latter available by advance reservation only).

Westhalten

AUBERGE DU CHEVAL BLANC
20 Rue de Rouffach
Tel: 89 47 01 16.
Closed Sunday evening and all day Monday.
This historic guest-house combines both the romance and the comforts of Alsace in its hotel and in its top-flight culinary offerings. From the wood-panelled guest room you can watch the cooks at work. Complete menu prices cost £10–25.

Gueberschwihr

BELLE-VUE
13 Rue des Forgerons.
Tel: 89 49 22 22.
Closed Thursday.
This restaurant has a very beautiful observation terrace with a view over vineyard-covered hills and village roofs. In addition to its excellent Alsatian cuisine this family operation also maintains a very pleasant hotel, with rooms costing from £20–45.

Rouffach

CHATEAU D'ISENBOURG
North of Rouffach.
Tel: 89 49 63 53.
Hardly any other restaurant in Alsace has such a commanding location – on a hill in the middle of vineyards. The title 'gourmet temple' would be an accurate description of the château. An exclusive hotel forms an appropriate complement for the Restaurant Les Tommeries. This ambience of course has its price: the outstanding complete gourmet menu costs in the region of £70; rooms are priced correspondingly at £50–100.

Eguisheim

CAVEAU D'EGUISHEIM
3 Place du Château Saint Léon.
Tel: 89 41 08 89.
Closed Tuesday evening and all day Wednesday.
Famous for its wine cellar which captures the quintessence of Alsatian *joie de vivre*. The best wines from the showcase village of Eguisheim sparkle in your glass; fine fish or lamb with equally divine herbs excite every olfactory nerve. There are, of course, complete meals starting at £15 on the menu, but if you want the highest pleasures, then shell out for the *Menu Degustation* at £45.

The Ecomusée

A museum village without a museum character – full of living tradition.

This open-air museum, located 12km (7½ miles) to the north of Mulhouse, is among the highlights of the French museum landscape. As many as 300,000 visitors find their way here each year. In 1989 the project was awarded the Europa Prize for Museum of the Year – with justice. Liveliness, authenticity and clarity are its guidelines. In the beginning of the 1970s the founder and director, Marc Grodwohl, began to save old Alsatian farmsteads from decay in the Sundgau. At first these were renovated in situ; later on, however, Grodwohl and his friends switched over to dismantling them; when, after a long search, the right plot of land was found, they reconstructed these farmsteads to create a museum village.

The goal of the museum is to give the visitor an impression of early village life, and to prevent old skills and traditions from falling into the realm of the forgotten. With over 60 buildings, dating from the 12th to the 19th centuries, a sense of historical continuity is evident and the museum portrays various trades which belonged to the life of a village. Besides the **farmsteads** the complex includes a **blacksmith's shop**, **wagon-building** and **shoe-makers' workshops**, an **oil-mill** and a **weaving shop**. In the fishermens' house from Artolsheim, originally built in 1561, there is an informative display on the life of the fisherman. A notice records the fact that René Christ pulled the last salmon from the Rhine in 1953. A photograph from 1937 shows a boy, by the name of Jeannot, with his first cigarette, given to him as a sign of his entrance into the world of men after catching his first fish – he is one of the men who advised the Ecomusée in the reconstruction.

Standing beside the fishermens' house is an old village tavern; standing between the two is the watch-tower that was built by a nobleman from Mulhouse. Various craftsmen can be watched as they work – you can also pass judgement on their level of technical development. An example of advanced technology – using renewable energy – is the **Vosges Sawmill**, dating to the early 20th century, which is powered by a large water-wheel some 6m (20ft) in diameter.

Another big attraction is the French **Salon Carousel**, from the year 1900,

with bar,
dance floor and plush and
leather booths – a real turn-of the century
'discotheque'. This work of art is valued at 11 million
francs. Children can do their rounds on the animal sculptures until
late autumn – in the winter the carousel is closed. In several of the
houses visitors can watch continuously running videotapes which
explain – in German and French – how to go about building a
tiled stove, a half-timbered house or an oven for baking bread.

The museum village also has a 'real' river at its disposal. The
water is diverted through a canal from the Thur. A wetland area is
being created in one of the tributaries running off the canal with
the aim of providing a marsh landscape. Visitors can take a 20-
minute barque ride on the river. Perhaps one of the storks that
live here will circle over you as you ride; there are now twelve
nests here. The storks are not the only animals: altogether there
are about 150 horses, pigs, goats and hens – everything that you
would expect to find in a real farming village.

The main theme of the Sunday and holiday presentations at the
Ecomusée is **agriculture**. Depending on the season of the year, different agricultural methods and religious festivals form the theme
for demonstrations and displays. Hay harvesting, tobacco curing,
grape gathering, summer laundry and wood cutting, distillation of
spirits and honey centrifuging – there is always something going
on on a Sunday. Soon there should also be a brewery and a
chocolate factory. They are both located on the canal, to which a
street will eventually be added displaying city buildings from the
close of the 19th century.

Finally, a **street-car** provides a connection to the industrial
monument, called the Kalamine Rodolphe, which is currently being
restored. Here there will be some 200 machines on display. Among
the most significant is a textile machine and an old printing press.
And, if the amount of traffic grows too much, old buses will be
used to help take some of the load off the street-car line.

The museum provides for bodily well-being with several restaurants; however, on the days with the heaviest crowds, the chances
are that you will wind up leaving with an empty stomach.

Opening hours are: November–March 11am–5pm; April, May
and October 10am–6pm; June through to the end of September
9am–7pm. Admission: adults 44 francs; children 16 francs.

Mulhouse

A tour through Mulhouse and its technical museums.

The industrial city of Mulhouse (pronounced *Moolooze*) with its 110,000 inhabitants is considered the ugly duckling among the three larger cities of Alsace. Tourists come here primarily because of the outstanding technical museums. This fact should not deter you from visiting: a two-hour tour of the city reveals that there are several interesting things to discover.

From a good distance, as you approach the city, you can see the symbol of Mulhouse – the **Europe Tower**. Here, the concrete sterility of 1960s architecture has left a gigantic monument to itself. Even so, there is a great view from high up in the tower's rotating restaurant. And, if you're sitting inside, at least you don't have to look at the tower.

Our tour begins at the tourist office in the **Avenue du Maréchal Foch**, not far from the train station. On the corner of the Place de la Républic are two terrace-cafés, **Le Moll** and **Rey**, in summer the meeting point of the Mulhouse 'scene'. In the **Avenue de Lattre de Tassigny** you can enjoy a relaxing breakfast – on Sundays as well – 100m (328ft) further on, in the *salon de thé* **Au Péché Mignon**. The almond croissants here are delicious. The **Rue de Sauvage** leads into the pedestrian zone. The **CCA**, a first-class *Charcuterie*

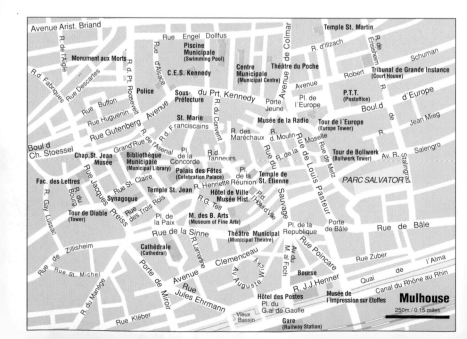

Mulhouse's former city hall

Alsacienne, caters to fans of sausages and meats.

At the **Place des Victoires** we turn off left in front of the fountain. After 200m (656ft) you are standing on the **Place de la Réunion**, the most attractive plaza in Mulhouse, from which, for tunately, the automobile should soon be banned. In 1909 the *Schweissdisse* was also banned; this statue of a half-naked worker, earning his bread by the sweat of his brow, was banished to the Place du Tivoli in the neighbourhood of the train station because of the protests of some influential citizens. This story is documented in Mulhouse's **Historical Museum**, located in the former city hall, a beautiful, richly painted Renaissance structure. It is worth taking a look at the council hall – in which the Mulhouse city council still holds meetings. In addition there are displays of archaeological material, folk art, traditional costumes, furniture and a collection of beautiful old toys.

In the 19th-century church of St **Etienne**, which is located diag-onally opposite the city hall, there are ten windows preserved from an older church of the 14th century. Next door to the city hall is the **Patisserie Jacques**, which offers some fine sweet morsels. Located on the left-hand side, at the end of **Rue Guillaume Tell** is the **Musée des Beaux Arts** – there is more than technology and industry in Mulhouse. Further on, in the **Rue Alfred Engel**, the AMC **Culture Centre** takes care of the more recent arts. The galleries host outstanding exhibitions of photography and other art.

Via the **Rue du Raisin** to the **Place de la Concorse** and then,

The Europe Tower

through an arched gateway dating to 1761, into the **Passage des Augustins** we proceed through crooked little streets to the Chapel St Jean. You can eat good vegetarian food at reasonable prices in the nearby **Tête de Chou** in Rue des Trois Rois.

From the Passage des Augustins we stroll into the **Rue de Lucelle**, the first street on the left. The **Chapel St Jean** displays 16th-century mural paintings as well as a collection of stone sculptures and gravestones. Next we walk along the Grand'Rue, passing by the library, and across diagonally to the left into the cul-de-sac. Up this street, on the right, is an unusual wall-painting and the **Terrasse des Gambrinus**, a tavern which is well known in Mulhouse for its immense assortment of beers and its generous helpings of food.

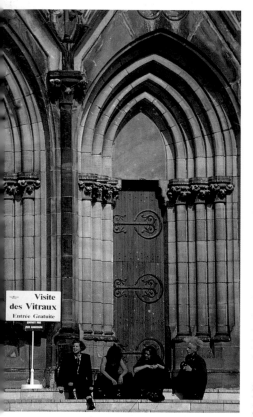

Visite des Vitraux
Entrée Gratuite

Shall we go to church?

Through a small, lovingly maintained park with a brook running through it we walk along past the remains of the old city wall. At the end of this mini-park we keep to the right and take the **Rue des Franciscains**. The restored **Cours des Chaines** shelters a culture and information centre; the interior terrace of the **Café des Arts** has a stage where, during the summer, dance and theatre productions as well as concerts take place. Nearby is yet another 'in' place: the **Greffier** at 16 Rue de la Loi.

Those besieged by a growling stomach can go up the Rue de l'Arsenal and look into the **Sauwadala**, where you can also get Alsatian dishes late at night. With the Rue des Tanneurs we are again coming close to the business centre. Located at No 15 Rue des Bons Enfants is the little restaurant called **Le Petit Zinc**. Here you can enjoy French cuisine at reasonable prices with friendly service.

Next we proceed straight through the modern shopping gallery, **La Cours de Maréchaux** and, after going through a passage, return to the Place de la Réunion. Good coffee is to be had at the **Arc** on Rue Henriette, and a fine wine tavern of the same name is located at No 9. Now we walk back to the plaza, and from there – via the Passage de l'Hotel de Ville – onto the Rue de la Sinne. The city theatre is located on the corner of the Avenue August Wicky; diagonally across from it is the fanciful hotel, **Le Parc**.

The Railway Museum

From here our path takes us back to the tourist office, the starting point of the tour. If you feel like it you can now drive to one or more of the city's diverse museums; the routes are – for the most part – well signposted.

Musée de l'Impression sur Etoffe: Eight million fabric patterns and designs are kept here; they are are exhibited in rotation since they cannot all be be displayed simultaneously. It is possible to trace the history of fabric printing from the 18th century to the present day. Because of their beauty, the fabrics of the Mulhouse manufacturers were once without competition. In addition you can see hand-printed materials from around the world.
3 Rue des Bonnes Gens.
Open daily June 1–August 31; 9am–6pm; otherwise daily except Tuesday 10am–noon and 2–6pm; admission: adults 22 francs; children, from age ten, 7 francs.

Le Musée de l'Automobile: You don't have to be an automobile fan to be enchanted with the Mulhouse car museum's collection of almost 500 old-timers. The museum presents an overview of 100 years of automotive history. Among the specimens to be seen here are Charlie Chaplin's Rolls Royce and the Bugatti *Coupé Napoleon* which belonged to Ettore Bugatti himself. Besides the collection of 123 Bugattis (the museum's founders, the Schlumpf brothers, were eventually bankrupted by their passion for collecting Bugatti cars) there are models from Mercedes, Peugeot, Ferrari, Maserati and other famous names. Some 350,000 visitors make the pilgrimage to this 'Louvre' of the automobile age every year.
192 Avenue de Colmar.
Open daily 10am–6pm; admission: adults 42 francs; children 19 francs.

The Car Museum

The **Railway Museum** is another high-point of Mulhouse's museum landscape. Parked on six sets of tracks are steam and electric locomotives, passenger cars and transport wagons, all providing an overview of the development of French railways. The oldest locomotive, a St Pierre with wooden-sheathed cylinders, was built in 1844. The luxurious Pullmann saloon cars (1926) prove that people knew how to travel in comfort 60 years ago. In the adjacent Omnimax cinema (separate admission) primarily technical films are presented on a 160 degree projection screen. The audience gets the feeling of being right in the middle of the action.
2 Rue Alfred Glehn.
Daily 9am–6pm; admission: adults 28 francs; children 12 francs.

Further Museums and Sightseeing Tips:

The **Wallpaper Museum**, 24 Rue Josué Hofer (in Rixheim, 4km (2½ miles) to the east of Mulhouse), has a collection of 130,000 kinds of wallpaper, which are displayed in rotation. Open daily except Tuesday 10am–noon and 2–6pm; admission: adults 22 francs; children 7 francs.

The **Maison de la Céramique** at 24 Rue Josué Hofer, is an old brick factory which has been renovated very tastefully – here you can see primarily ceramic exhibits. The displays cover craft pottery and modern industrial production. Visitors can watch potters at work and see a changing display of the work of local artists. Tuesday–Saturday 10am–noon and 2–6pm; Friday until 7pm.

The **Zoo** (111 Avenue de la Première Division DB (south entrance); 1 Avenue de la 9E DIC (north entrance), with its more than 1,100 animals, also serves as a botanic garden. Its landscape design is very spacious – it is considered the most beautiful animal park in France. Open daily 9am–5pm; in the summer until 7pm; admission: adults 25 francs; children 12 francs.

Restaurants

Aux Caves du Vieux Couvent
23 Rue du Couvent
Tel: 89 46 28 79
Closed Sunday and Monday afternoon.
A wine tavern in old Mulhouse in which you can enjoy regional cuisine at good prices.

Gambrinus
5 Rue Franciscains
Tel: 89 66 18 65
Closed Sunday lunch time.
Mulhouse 'beer temple' with an extraordinary selection of fermented barley-juice. Also simple food in ample portions.

Le Monastir
4 Rue de la Filature.
Tel: 89 42 94 44.
Closed Monday.
If you're looking for an alternative to Alsatian cuisine, then you're well advised to give this little Tunisian restaurant a try. Inexpensive, good, and with pleasant service.

La Poste
7 Rue Général de Gaulle, in the Mulhouse suburb of Riedesheim
Tel: 89 44 07 71.
Closed all day Sunday and Tuesday evening.
One of the best restaurants in the southern Alsace region. Chef Jean-Marc Kieny enchants his guests with fresh dishes which he prepares daily, he takes his inspiration from nearby Switzerland, and gourmets will find pleasure in the wines and desserts alone. A five-course menu costs around £25.

La Tonnelle
61 Rue du Maréchal Joffre in Riedesheim.
Tel: 89 54 25 77.
Closed Saturday afternoon and all day Sunday.
The creations of Jean-Marie Hirtzlin are evidence of the masterpieces which he learned while working for Paul Bocuse, the high priest of nouvelle cuisine. For around £45 you are served such delicacies as guinea hen with finely diced white cabbage. A selection of 240 wines might make your choice somewhat challenging.

Hotels

Salvator
29 Passage Central.
Tel: 89 45 28 32.
A good solid mid-range hotel.
Rooms: £25–35.

Hotel du Parc
26 Rue de la Sinne.
Tel: 89 66 12 22.
A turn-of-the-century luxury hotel with latter-day comforts. Rooms start at £70 per night; if you wish you can also reserve a luxury suite for £325.

The Southern Vosges

From Guebwiller to the Murbach Monastery; the Vosges; Le Markstein and Grand Ballon; the Vieil Armand Battlefield; on to Thann.

The highway from Mulhouse to Guebwiller leads you through the potash basin. Abandoned mining towers, half-decayed warehouses and huge slag heaps are evidence – much to the astonishment of the unprepared visitor – that besides the romance of half-timbered architecture and all that comes with it, there is also a certain industrial romance to the Alsace. Not far from here, located near Pulversheim, is the highly recommended Ecomusée open-air museum (see Tour 11: *The Ecomusée*).

Guebwiller is located at the entrance to the **Florival** – or Valley of Flowers – named after its abundant vineyards. The grapes grow right up to the main street of the town. Until the 18th century this small city lived from winemaking; after that, textile and machine industries were added. The neoclassical **Notre Dame** church is worth looking at – it is the only building of this style in Alsace. From there you can amble up the main street towards the town centre. Half-timbered romance is with us again. Diagonally across from the antiquated city hall is **Pâtisserie Christmann** – known even beyond the limits of the town for its excellent croissants and other sweet delicacies. Fortified, we continue our stroll up the Rue de la République; soon the richly figured ornamentation of the church of **St Léger** appears on the right-hand side. This is the last great example of romantic building in Alsace.

Guebwiller is amply blessed with interesting churches: the **Dominican Church**, with its Gothic wall paintings, is especially famous – far beyond the Alsace – for its unusually fine acoustics. On the first Saturday of the summer months outstanding classical concerts take place here. One son of the city – ceramic maker Theodore Deck – has also become well-known for the glazes he has developed. About 150m (500ft) from the city hall towards Notre Dame, in a side-street off the Rue de la Republique, the entire wall

Guebwiller's renowned
Dominican church

Guebwiller

of a house is covered with a portrait in his memory. You can also examine some of Deck's works in the **Florival Museum** (Monday–Friday, afternoons only; Saturday and Sunday, 10am–noon also); the beautiful old tiled wall which was discovered recently during the remodelling of an industrial villa and transfered to the museum is alone worth the entrance fee.

In a side-valley only a few kilometres to the north of Guebwiller is the Monastery Church of Murbach, the highpoint of this tour. Founded in the 8th century, it was the political, economic and cultural centre of the Upper Alsace. The monks knew where to live well. This picture-book valley, a place of dreamlike beauty, is also well supplied with restaurants and hotels offering guests every comfort. You can humour your palate in the **Restaurant Saint Barnabé**, several kilometres before the abbey. If you only want a snack, turn into the **Auberge de l'Abbaye**, only a few hundred metres from the monastery church. Leave your car here at the parking area and go by foot to the church, which is one of the most beautiful Romanesque structures in Alsace. About halfway there a crossing path on the right-hand side leads you, after about five minutes, to the little **Loretto Chapel**. Tourists rarely stray this far and you might even surprise a pheasant.

Next we head along the main road towards the Markstein. After a few kilometres you arrive at **Lautenbach**. If you want a vivid portrait of life in this region of Alsace you should read *The Lindens of Lautenbach*, which tells of the childhood of a young Alsatian between the World Wars and his inner strife between German and French identities. In Lautenbach do not miss the **collegiate church**; at its entrance is a remarkable relief – the carving includes a grinning witch who stares down at all visitors.

Next we continue towards the peaks of the Vosges. If your

Guebwiller is surrounded by vineyards

stomach is already protesting you can stop off at one of the numerous Fermes Auberges whose signs line our route. At the **Lodge Gustiberg** a mailbox has switched functions – it is now a bird's nest, and an epigram on the hand-painted route map makes it clear that people here still have a special relationship with nature. It says: "The mountains deserve no mediocrity". If you are wearing high-heels you are better off skipping this excursion.

You can also get a reasonably priced snack in the **Restaurant Belle Vue** on the Markstein. This restaurant has a right to bear its name; at 1,200m (3,937ft) it has one of the most beautiful panoramic views in the Vosges. The view is also dreamlike from the **Grand Ballon**, which at 1,424m (4,672ft) is the highest peak in the Vosges (you can get there in about 20 minutes). On a clear day – especially in autumn and winter, as well as some days in summer – you can see from here all the way to the Alps. If, after such long views, you don't really feel like returning to the lower levels of the valley, then the idyllically located **Hotel/Restaurant Goldmatten** is recommended (watch out for the direction signs after turning off in the direction of Thann). The rooms are simple and very quiet.

Instead of driving on further to Thann right away, you might take a quick excursion to the **Vieil Armand**, a World War I battlefield. The fighting around the mountain lasted for years, and 30,000 soldiers are thought to have lost their lives. Today there is a French national monument here. A small museum displays photographs from the period of the battle, as well as German and French armoury.

Now we drive roughly 5km (3 miles) back to the intersection and after 20 minutes arrive in **Thann**. Along with Strasbourg cathedral, the **Collegiate Church** is among the most significant Gothic works in the Alsace. In the **Brasserie République** there are occasional jazz concerts. The **Historical Museum** is housed in former 16th-century granary. Here there are many photographs and other reminders of the Nazi occupation.

If your legs are still holding out, you can take the 30-minute climb up to the Engelsburg (Angels' Castle). When the castle was blasted in the 17th century a portion of the tower fell on to its side and is today called the 'Witches Eye'. Finally, if you really enjoy driving, then we recommend that you take the detour over the beautiful **Route Joffre** to **Masevaux**. From there you reach the superhighway via Lauw and Geuwenheim.

The direct route from Thann goes over the high-speed road to Mulhouse. The warning signs *affaisement minier* refer to the fact that the road is full of potholes and areas of subsidence caused by potash mining works – enough to drive road builders, and nearby home-owners, to despair.

Restaurants

Murbach

SAINT BARNABE
25 Rue de Murbach in Buhl.
Tel: 89 76 92 15.
Closed in winter, Sunday evening and Monday.
A top-flight guest house with a magnificent ambience. Specialities include goose liver and pike. For an appealing complete meal the gourmet should plan on spending at least £20.

Lac du Ballon

FERME-AUBERGE DU GUSTIBERG
Turn off past Lautbachzell onto the D430 to the Lac du Ballon. The entrance is then signposted.
Tel: 89 74 05 01.
Open from mid-April to mid-November.
In the nearby vacation and recreation center (Tel: 89 76 84 65) groups can book rooms for the night. This is an ideal starting and destination point for hikes around the foot of the Grand Ballon.

Markstein

FERME-AUBERGE DU HAHNEN-BRUNNEN
At the Col de Hahnenbrunnen on the Route des Crêtes.
Tel: 89 77 68 99.
Open from June to September.
Located at an altitude of 1,180m (3,870ft); a wild and romantic mountain farmstead with simple, hearty specialities of the Vosges.

Hotels

Grand Ballon

HOTEL LE GRAND BALLON
Tel: 89 76 83 35
A rustic hotel and meeting place for hikers at the highest point in the Alsace. Good restaurant with regional cuisine. Rooms from £10–20.

Goldbach

GOLDENMATT
On the D13 between Grand Ballon and Thann.
Tel: 89 82 32 86.
A dreamily located mountain hotel with restaurant. Very popular, so often fully booked, but rooms are £20–35.

TOUR 14

In the Gentle Sundgau

A round-tour from Mulhouse through the Sundgau and over the Alsatian Juras to Ferrette and Altkirch.

The southernmost part of the Alsace, the Sundgau, is often portrayed as something of a poor relation; the area simply can't compete with the conglomeration of cultural monuments in Strasbourg or Colmar. If, however, you are looking for relief from the hubbub of tourism and a day's break from culture, then this green, hilly and charming landscape is just the thing. 'Poor relations' frequently have the habit of not being too overwhelming – in this way their hidden charms are that much more appreciated.

The D21 passes by the Mulhouse railway station on its route toward **Bruebach**. There is a good view over Mulhouse and the surrounding region from the **Belvédère Observation Tower**. Just be-

yond the zoo, follow the direction signs for the *Mémorial des Déportés*. This monument was erected in to commemorate the *Malgré Armee* of World War I.

The **Sundgau** starts just a few kilometres to the south of Mulhouse. In the first village the bleached-out inscription '*Gastwirtschaft*' on a house here reminds us that, for some fifty years, Alsace was part of the German Reich. In Steinbrunn-le-Bas we turn off to the left towards Folgensbourg. Located on the left-hand side, not far beyond the village exit, is the **Moulin du Kaegy**, a former mill built in 1565. It has since been turned into a restaurant and lies in the middle of enchanting natural surroundings, away from the road. Gourmets are not sparing in their praise of this place but the prices are correspondingly inflated.

Next we continue through some typical Sundgau villages. To the east of the road we are accompanied by the mountain ridge of the Black Forest; at **Helfrantzkirch** you can make out the Alsatian Juras to the south. In **Oltingue** the farm and home-museum (**Maison du Sundgau**) – located in a 16th-century auberge – conveys an impression of everyday life in the Sundgau in times gone by (open from mid-May–mid-October on Thursday and Saturday 3 6pm; otherwise Sunday 2 5pm).

Snacks can be had in the **Salon du Thé Oltinguette**. The more brave among you might try the sauerkraut ice-cream which proprietor Tony Hartmann has created. He works hard as chairman of the Sauerkraut Brotherhood to develop new dimensions for the Alsatian 'national' dish.

Ferrette

Going through **Wolschwiller** the road now leads us to **Kiffis** in the heights of the Alsatian Juras. The Swiss border is now very close. On the way to Lucell you pass several mostly unoccupied border posts; the road even goes a short way into Swiss territory (the course of the border is determined by the River Lucelle; when the road is on the other side, then you are in Switzerland).

With its 53 inhabitants, Lucelle is the smallest community in the upper Alsace – the Swiss border also runs through the village. Here a famous Cistercian abbey (1123–1790) once stood; only the gate and a fountain survived. Even so, this picturesque town, with its little lake, can't complain of a shortage of guests at weekends.

At the turn-off to **Winkel**, where the source of the Ill River is to be found, benches and splendid views invite us to rest. The little town of **Ferrette** is also worth a stop. The **castle ruins** have a beautiful view (ten minutes on foot from the city hall). If you feel like a bit more exercise, then you might hike the half hour to the **Grotte des Nain** – the Dwarf's Cave. According to tradition the fairies used to live here. They were very generous to the local people and helped them with their more unpleasant tasks. This enviable situation was destroyed by the curiosity of a young girl who absolutely had to know what kind of feet were hidden under the

In the Sundgau

fairies' long robes – she spread fine sand in front of their cave, on which appeared the footprints of geese and goats. Since this break in trust angered the little beings, they withdrew their help. Consequently the residents of Ferrette have to do all their own work again. The visitor will be glad of this, however: there are five restaurants at the service of hungry guests. The front terrace of the **Hotel Felseneck** is a very pleasant place to relax. At **Collin** you can dine and stay overnight.

Our route now continues to **Feldbach**. It is well worth looking into the lovingly renovated 12th-century Romanesque church here. Take the first street to the right after the traffic roundabout. **Hirsingue** and **Hirtzbach** are pretty, flower-ornamented villages; in **Carspach** the food in the **Couronne** is excellent. The town of **Altkirch** (6,000 residents) is located in the centre of the Sundgau

region on a hill overlooking the Ill Valley. The neo-Gothic fountain, the city hall, several historic houses and **Notre Dame** church are all worth a look. From the church there is a beautiful view over the valley. In addition, the **Sundgau Museum** displays traditional costumes, the works of the painter Jean-Jacques Henner, archeological finds and folk-art (open daily except Monday 3–5.30pm in July and August; otherwise only Sunday afternoon).

In Froeningen the **Auberge de Froeningen** is an attractive place to round off the day with a fine meal. The service and atmosphere are pleasant and friendly. If after having eaten – you don't feel like driving anymore, you can spend a pleasant night here.

The Sundgau is an ideal region for cycling. At the train station in Mulhouse you can rent a bike (although they sometimes leaves something to be desired). A two-day tour with overnight lodging in Ferrette is available (following

Sundgauer anglers

the same route described for our car journey). The ascent to Kiffis is included – it can be done, and the ride downhill is reward for all the fatigue. The less sporty among us can drive straight to Ferrette. From there, on the next day you go via Mooslargue, Seppoisle-Haut, Dannemarie, Hagenbach, Galfingue and then back to Mulhouse. There are numerous fish ponds and picturesque villages along the way, with the Vosges providing the backdrop.

Restaurants

Steinbrunn-le-Bas

MOULIN DE KAEGY
Tel: 89 81 30 34.
Closed Sunday evening and all day Monday.
A fine restaurant in a beautifully renovated old mill which originally dates to the mid-16th century. Gourmets (among them many Swiss visitors) will gasp with pleasure at the combination of the setting and fine food. If you are not averse to laying out £30 – for the cheapest complete menu – then you should reserve ahead, since the Kaegy is often fully booked.

Lutter

AUBERGE PAYSANNE
24 Rue Wollschwiller
Tel: 89 40 71 67.
Closed Monday.
A simple rustic spot with classic regional cuisine and reasonably priced overnight accommodation. Rooms: £10–20.

Citroën rally in the Vosges

Ferrette

AU CHEVAL BLANC
1 Rue Léon-Lehmann.
Tel: 89 40 41 30.
Closed Saturday evening and all day Monday.
A simple place that will appeal to all who like a rustic atmosphere and inexpensive food.

Froeningen

AUBERGE DE FROENINGEN
2 Route d'Illfurth.
Tel: 89 25 48 48.
Closed Sunday evening and all day Monday.
A warm and hearty welcome, separate rooms for smoking and non-smoking guests, and an earthy – yet creative – culinary approach are the trademarks of this auberge.

Complete lunch menus start at £10. In the evening the Menu *La Bombance* for £30 is recommended. Afterward you can bed down in the beautiful hotel (as long as it is not fully booked – advance reservation is advisable). Rooms cost £25–35.

Hotels

COLLIN
4 Rue du Chateau.
Tel: 89 40 40 72.
A family-run business offering rooms with solid comfort and southern Alsatian regional cuisine. In the restaurant you can try the fried carp – a speciality of the Sundgau. You almost have to dine here if you want to stay overnight: without dining you are unlikely to get a room. Rooms cost £15–20.

Dining Ex

The reputation of Alsatian food is, belatedly, beginning to earn the respect it deserves. One traveller, when asked where he would rather eat – in Germany or in France – is said to have answered: "In Germany you get a lot, but it's not good; In France it's good – but you don't get much; but in the Alsace, it's both good and plentiful."

Even so, some unconvinced observers still claim that the cuisine of the Alsace lives mainly off quantity and that its quality leaves something to be desired. The same critics say that the many dining-tourists who stream in to Alsace at the weekends from the neighbouring German province of Baden would be better off staying at home and indulging in their local cooking (which, by the way, is certainly not to be scorned). It has to be said that this sort of critic is now in the minority, and is only right in one or two exceptional cases, since no region lacks its black sheep. When the famed German food critic Wolfgang Siebeck published his ten-part summer series on his culinary explorations in the Alsatian 'wonderland', in *Zeitmagazin*, it was yet more proof that the gastronomical qualities of the Alsace region consist of more than pure myth.

Whether you are an aristocratic connoisseur, an occasional gourmet, a disciple of nouvelle cuisine, or simply an enchanted admirer and consumer of the French dining culture – however you classify yourself, if you like food, you'll like the Alsace. There is something for every taste and every wallet: the rustic cooking of the fermes auberges, classic French cuisine, carefully prepared regional dishes, the latest achievements of nouvelle cuisine or, perhaps, the evolving combination of regional tradition with innovation. And even though the representatives of the American mass junk-food culture, the McDonalds and Burger Kings and whatever they call themselves, have also begun to invade the romantic half-timbered villages, there are still homely little wine-taverns *en masse*. The long gastronomic tradition, which Alsace can look back upon, has proven itself strong enough – thank goodness – to hold its ground against chewing-gum and ketchup imperialism.

In recent time the gastronomic image of Alsace in the rest of France has improved considerably. The region was, of course, already recognised for its economic significance; not, however, for its culinary excellence until very recently. Thus, the wine specialist of the famous **Auberge de l'Ill** was voted the world's best sommelier in 1989, and the French gourmet 'papacy' has newly elevated Emile Jung's **Crocodile** into the three-star heavens, where the Haeberlins' Auberge de l'Ill already shines. In itself, the highly official exit sign on the superhighway pointing the way to this gustatory temple speaks for the renown of this most noble of auberges. Where else do you see state advertising on behalf of a restaurant? Despite the horrendous prices – quality has its price – it is extremely rare to get a table at the Haeberlin's establishment without prior reservation. But, if you do not want to spend between 350 and 500 francs for a complete menu, or if the tables are already fully booked, there are plenty of other opportunities to indulge in gourmet delights in Alsace.

Dining Traditions

Despite certain similarities which still exist between Alsace and Germany, dining customs in the Alsace are very French. This will be immediately obvious in the mornings, when the hungry guest stares disappointedly at a miserable little piece of baguette with butter and jam – the Alsatians, like most of the French, are not big champions in this arena. You might as well adjust to it and make the most of the meagre breakfast – in the course of the day you will have plenty of chance to appease your hungry stomach.

Lunch is served between noon and two o'clock. In many smaller restaurants and some *salons de thé* there are reasonably priced daily specials – the *plat du jour*. Many French have a two-hour lunchbreak. If they don't go home and don't have a work's cafeteria they eat in restaurants, which are often full as a result. The evening meal – usually a multi-course menu – is served between 7pm and 10pm. In rural districts and smaller towns, however, you may find it impossible to order hot food after 9pm. It is usually fruitless to search for an open restaurant between the main dining times.

As is usual in France, a table is assigned to you by the waiting staff. Bread is served with meals and no-one will be shocked if you use the bread to mop up food and clean your plate. If you eat out with friends or acquaintances, plan on paying with a single cheque and dividing the costs later on. It is unusual to pay separately in France; a request of this nature might drive some waiters to despair. You should also consider the following a basic rule of thumb: the more deeply you have to reach into your wallet, the smaller the portions will be. As a rule, however, the higher prices will be compensated for with quality.

The tradition of taking coffee or tea in the afternoons is unknown in France, so cakes and such are normally served as a dessert. If you do not want to give up your domestic traditions, however, you can certainly enjoy coffee and cake either in a *salon de thé* or a *patisserie*.

Choucroute garni

Regional Dishes

Baeckeoffe: A layered casserole with various kinds of meat, potatoes, onions and white wine. This dish was originally cooked in bakers' ovens. Because of the long time needed for its preparation (three hours) the *baeckeoffe* must often be ordered ahead of time.

Choucroute: Sauerkraut – a very hearty Alsatian 'national' dish with copious amounts of added meat. The classic *choucroute* includes a special variety of ham with bacon and smoked pork loin and shoulder; it is cooked in white wine and served with boiled potatoes. For several years now the 'Sauerkraut Brotherhood' has been trying to modernise the dish by serving sauerkraut as a side-dish with fish and other light dishes. The chairman of the Brotherhood, Tony Hartmann, has even created sauerkraut ice-cream in his endeavours to develop new dimensions for this dish. It's worth a try if you are visiting his Salon du Thé in Oltingue.

Coq au Riesling: Chicken pieces in Riesling wine; served most often with *spaetzle*, the tiny dumplings of German tradition.

Estomac de Porc Farci: Stuffed stomach of pig.

Fleischnaecka: Meat boiled in stock (usually beef) rolled up like a snail in noodle dough.

Kugelhupf: Apple pancakes, often served as a dessert with ice cream.

Matelot: A ragout made of four or five kinds of fish. It usually consists of pike, tench, perch, trout and eel and is cooked in a white wine sauce which is enriched with cream, cognac, herbs and garlic.

Munster cheese: A soft raw cheese made of fresh cow's milk which has a strong odour and is sometimes spiced with caraway or aniseed. The cheese is formed into small discs and ripened in a well-aired cellar for about a month. It is believed to have been invented by 8th-century monks. Today, Munster cheese is made by some two dozen farms in the Munster valley, several of which have rustic restaurants attached.

Flammekueche or **Tarte Flambée:** An Alsatian pizza of thinly rolled bread dough, curds, chopped onions and bacon. This dish originally came from Northern Alsace, but nowadays it is also offered in the south. Normally the *tarte flambée* is brought to the table on a large wooden platter and divided by the guests. Waiters will continue to bring more until you tell them to stop.

Pâté de foie gras: Goose-liver *pâté*. An Alsatian speciality which was invented a good 200 years ago by a chef in Lorraine. The poor goose must suffer for this very delicious dish. The widely criticized practice of force-feeding the geese does not seem to bother French gourmets.

Pot au feu: A beef stew with many vegetables.

Presskopf: Pickled meat in aspic.

Quiche Lorraine: A hearty pie which – as is obvious from the name – originated in Lorraine. It consists of eggs and cream with bacon and cheese laid on top, and is often eaten along with wine in taverns.

Rognons: Kidneys served either pickled or with cream.

Schiffala: Smoked pork shoulder served with horseradish sauce or with mustard.

Sorbet au Gewurztraminer: Lemon sorbet with a shot of Gewurztraminer wine.

Tarte à l'Oignon: Onion pie.

Waedele: Leg of pork.

Shopping

One point should be stated at the outset: there are no great shopping bargains to be had in Alsace. Value-added-tax is high in France and, anyway, France was never an inexpensive country to shop in. There are, however, plenty of opportunities to browse around in **flea markets** and **antique shops**. North African immigrants bring their exotic and colourful wares to the markets. One of the best is the **Marché du Canal Couvert** in Mulhouse with its oriental bazaar atmosphere; it is held on Tuesday, Thursday and Saturday; another market is held on the **Boulevard de la Marne** on Saturday and Tuesday. You can check out the dates of the numerous flea markets in the regional press. Enthusiasts of Asian cuisine can load up on sauces, spices and such at good prices in a number of shops which are operated by Vietnamese exiles. They are mainly found in Strasbourg and Mulhouse.

Germanic order prevails to a great extent in the local laws – originating from the Kaiser period – which means that stores are closed on Sundays. But we would not be in France if a few exceptions were not tolerated. On Sundays and holidays there are quite a number of small corner stores whose mostly Arabic proprietors serve the local population in their own enterprising manner. As a rule, however, you have to pay a bit more for this service. Otherwise, **retail businesses** are open weekdays and Saturdays from 8am–noon and from 2pm–6 or 7pm. Some stores are closed on Monday morning. Supermarkets usually open continuously from 9am–6.30 or 7pm; on Saturdays until 6pm. Some of the large shopping centres on the city outskirts stay open late on weekdays usually until 8pm.

Fans of delicacies will find what they are looking for in Strasbourg's gourmet supermarket **Galérie Gourmande**, located between the railroad station and Kléber Place in the shopping centre Centres Halles. Things are by no means cheaper here than at home, but you will find many tempting and exotic foods and specialities.

Alsace is the cradle of goose-liver pâté. It was invented in the autumn of 1783 by the head chef of the military governor; since then *pâté de foie gras de Strasboug* has become popular all over France and far beyond. If you are planning to load up on Alsatian goose-liver specialities you should know that they are, for the most part, only *processed* in the Alsace; the raw product originates frequently from Eastern Europe or Israel. Second problem: the animals are force-fed – thus animal lovers will want to abstain. Gourmets should know that duck-liver *pâté* takes a smaller bite out of your vacation budget than the goose-liver version – though the flavour is somewhat more robust.

Apropos saving: photographers should – as far as is feasible – pack sufficient film and, if you are coming in from Germany, it is a good idea to fill up your petrol tank before the border. The French government likes to bleed its citizens with indirect taxes. On the other hand, some things are relatively inexpensive: it is worthwhile to buy wine, champagne, and *Eau de Vie* – a clear digestif which comes in raspberry, cherry, yellow plum or pear-flavoured liquors. Cigarettes are also cheaper than elsewhere in northern Europe, especially if you like the strong taste of Gitanes or Gaulloises.

Alsatiques is the name given to publications that deal with the folklore, art and history of Alsace. The books are usually available in several European languages. You can find Alsatiques in all bookshops. You should watch for the quality designation *Souvenir de France, Alsace Authentique* when buying momentoes such as pottery, wood carvings, leatherwork, knitted wares, printed scarves or puppets with traditional costumes. The label bears a stylised French rooster and is your guarantee of a genuine example of Alsatian workmanship.

Local baking in the Ecomusée

Calendar of Special Events

APRIL

Snail racing in Osenbach near Colmar. In this breathtaking competition, snails 'race' toward their goal over a half-metre (17 inch) track. Right next to the races you can consume the poor critters' brothers and sisters with garlic butter. For information telephone 89 47 00 26.
Narcissus Festival in Géradmar.

MAY

Ecology Fair in Rouffach: the big rendezvous for the Greens and other members of the Alsatian ecological scene. Several hundred stands with naturally made products such as wine, bread, cheese, teas, candles, etc. Also an extensive side-programme including games, music, speeches and discussions. Tel: 89 49 62 54.

Lily of the Valley Festival in Neu Breisach and Wissembourg.

JUNE

Rose Festival in Saverne: glorious flower displays, folklore presentations and a programme of entertainment in the park. Tel: 88 19 08 59.

Pentecost: International folklore procession in Wissembourg.

Beginning of June: Kugelhopf Festival in Ribeauvillé: in a colourful parade a gigantic ring cake is drawn through the town. Tel: 89 73 62 22.

21 June: the *Fête de la Musique* is celebrated throughout France – a huge musical festival with free concerts in the streets. The action is provided by both amateurs and professionals.

24 June: Summer solstice festival: huge fires are set ablaze to celebrate the longest day of the year. Some communities also hold the *Fête de St Jean* several days earlier or later.

30 June: Fir-tree celebration in Thann. Fireworks, concerts and a folk festival. In memory of Bishop Theobaldus, who lived in the 12th century, a huge fire with ingeniously prepared fir trees is set alight. An impressive sight. Tel: 89 37 96 20.

JULY

On the **evening before 14 July** – the French national holiday – there are huge fireworks displays. The most impressive is in Strasbourg. In Mutzig thousands of onlooker participate in a traditional procession of the revolutionary *sans cullotes.*

Wine Festival in Barr with folklore groups and dancing: one of the oldest wine festivals in the region. Tel: 88 08 94 30.

End of July: In Kintzheim wine flows from a fountain at a big village festival – unfortunately not a permanent state of affairs.

AUGUST

Beer Festival in the Alsatian brewing capital of Schiltgenheim near Strasbourg.

'The Wedding of our friend Fritz' in Marlenheim. The *ami Fritz* was a confirmed bachelor who finally did get married – a character from a historical novel by Emil Erckmann and Alessandre Chatrian (1864). The celebration includes performances by numerous folk-groups. Tel: 88 87 51 09.

Wine Fair in Colmar with numerous different events: folklore, pop-music, cabaret and theatre. With its 500 varieties of wine this is the largest fair of its kind in the region. Tel: 89 41 60 00.

Battle of the Flowers in Sélestat: a procession of flowers with folklore groups and fireworks, an event which, in 1990, drew much of attention as a result of a daring poster by the Alsatian artist Tomi Ungerer. Family organizations and folklore groups protested against the poster, which featured a sparsely clothed Alsatian woman riding on a gorilla. The tumult over the poster could only be to the benefit of the organisers, since the 'Flower Battle' is now known throughout France and Germany. Tel: 88 92 02 66.

Hops Festival in Haguenau: includes an international folklore festival. Tel: 88 73 30 41.

Medieval Market in Wissembourg: authentically styled market in the historic city centre including costumed craftspeople, traders and singers. Tel: 88 94 10 11.

SEPTEMBER

Pipers' Day in Ribeauvillé: big, colourful parade with musicians and folklore presentations. Tel: 89 73 60 26.

Bread Festival in Michelbas-le-Haut (in the Sundgau): everything revolves around the production of bread.

What to Practical Information

TRAVEL ESSENTIALS

When to Go
The most pleasant time for a trip to Alsace is spring or autumn. The climate is mild but you should bring along warm things as well as light clothing. The temperatures can vary sharply from one day to the next. In the summer it can be very hot and humid. Winter on the Rhine river-plain often brings dense banks of fog with it.

Driving
The speed limit on the autoroutes is 130kmh (80mph) in dry conditions and 110kmh (68mph) when it is wet; on national highways (*Route Nationale*) 110kmh (68mph); on the smaller highways (*Route Départmentale*) 90kmh (56mph); on country roads (*Voie Ordinaire*) and in towns 60kmh (38mph) – as long as there are no other speed limits posted!

At night you are only allowed to drive with side-lights on in well-illuminated streets.

To park in a blue zone (*Zone Bleue*) you need a parking disk which shows your time of arrival.

Unless your car is diesel powered, it is worth filling up across the border in Germany. Petrol costs quite a bit more in France because of higher indirect taxes. Many Alsatians drive to Germany to buy their fuel. Lead-free petrol is not as widely available as in many European coutries, though the

situation is improving. If you have problems, the German and Swiss borders are not far away.

Car rental firms can be found in all the larger cities. Those with the biggest networks are Avis, Europcar and Hertz.

Car Accidents
So long as no-one is injured, the damage and course of events resulting in

businesses and restaurants accept Swiss francs and German marks. Credit cards are in wide use in France. At a number of bank ATMs you can also get French francs up to a maximum of around £130 with a Eurocheque card.

Tourist Information

Office Départmental du Tourisme du Bas-Rhin (Lower Alsace)
67061 Srasbourg CX, 9 Rue du Dome.
Tel: 88 22 01 02.

Association Départmentale Du Tourisme du Haut-Rhin (Upper Alsace)
68006 Colmar CX,
9 Rue Bruat.
Tel: 89 23 21 11.

Office du Tourisme Strasbourg
10 Place Gutenberg.
Tel: 88 32 57 07.

Office du Tourisme Colmar
4 Rue Unterlinden.
Tel: 89 41 02 29.

Office du Tourisme Mulhouse
9 Avenue du Maréchal Foch.
Tel: 89 45 68 31.

the accident have to be filled out on the insurance form by the affected parties *themselves* – the police are not responsible. If you are worried about language problems then obtain a multilingual European accident report form from your insurance company.

Maps
Michelin map No 87 Vosges–Alsace (1:200,000 scale) is excellent, and it is the cheapest on sale in Alsace. Clearly laid out, it includes all the tourist information you are likely to need.

Railway Stations (SNCF)
Strasbourg
  Information: 88 22 50 50.
  Reservations: 88 32 07 51.
Colmar
  Information: 89 24 50 50.
  Reservations: 89 23 17 00.
Mulhouse
  Information: 89 46 50 50.
  Reservations: 89 45 62 83.

Airports
Basel-Mulhouse, 30km (19 miles) from Mulhouse. Tel: 89 69 00 00.
Colmar-Houssen. Tel: 89 23 31 23.
Strazbourg-Entzheim, 13km (8 miles) from the city centre. Tel: 88 78 40 99.

Money Matters
The majority of banks are open Monday–Friday 9–11.30am/12.30pm and again 1.30pm/2pm–4pm/5pm. Some are closed Monday, but are open Saturday mornings. In the railway stations in Mulhouse and Strasbourg the change booth is also open at weekends. Many

ACCOMMODATION

Camping
You can camp anywhere you want to in the wild as long as there are no signs expressly forbidding it. You must follow the sanitary and police rules in doing so. Even if a night in a tent in the Vosges far away from civilization has its decided attractions, camping fans will also find a whole series of official campgrounds. Lists of them are available from the *Federation Francaise de Camping et Caravaning*, 78 Rue de Rivoli, F75004 Paris or at the *Touring Club de France*, 11 Rue de la Division Leclerc, F67000 Strasbourg, Tel: 88 32 72 63.

Youth Hostels

Strasbourg: 9 Rue de l'Auberge de Jeunesse (Montagne Verte city district). Tel: 88 30 26 46.
Colmar: 7 Rue Saint Niklas. Tel: 89 41 33 08.
Mulhouse: 37 Rue de l'Illberg. Tel: 89 42 63 28.
Saint Marie-aux-Mines: 21 Rue Reber. Tel: 89 58 75 74.
Grandfontaine (7km/5 miles northwest of Schirmeck): Les Miniéres.

HEALTH & EMERGENCIES

Emergency Telephone Numbers
Police: 17.
Fire Department (*pompiers*): 18.
Roadway Assistance (*touring secours*): 87 69 12 39/1 45 00 42 95.
Telephone Information: 12.

BUSINESS HOURS & HOLIDAYS

Businesses and Banks
Supermarkets are usually open on Monday to Sunday from 9.30am to at least 6.30pm in the evening, longer in the more built-up areas. On Sunday and holidays it is possible to shop in the morning in some supermarkets and almost all bakeries. On weekdays small businesses take a long mid-day break from 12.30pm–2/4pm.

Banks are open from Monday to Friday between 9.30am and noon as well as 2–4.30pm. In Strasbourg and Mulhouse you can also change money or cash Eurocheques on Sundays and holidays at the railway stations. Visitors with Swiss francs or German marks can use them almost everywhere in the tourist centres without difficulty. The exchange rates are reasonable.

Holidays
1 January, Good Friday, Easter Monday, 1 May, Ascension, Whit Monday, 15 August, All Saints' Day and 25–26 December.

French National Holidays: 8 May (Armistice 1945); 11 November (Armistice 1918); 14 July (Bastille Day).

COMMUNICATION & MEDIA

Language
The Alsatians are linguistically adroit and many of them, especially the youger generation, speak at least some English. You will make a good impression if you try to make yourself understood in French. The number of German speakers is constantly diminishing, though you can get by with it quite well in most shops and restaurants.

Postal Service
The post offices in France are marked by signs reading *PTT or P-et-T*.
Hours: Monday to Friday 9am–7pm and Saturday 8am–4pm.
Postage stamps are also available in tobacco shops.
Letters and postcards up to 20g cost 2.30 francs within the European Community; to Switzerland and Austria 2.50 francs. Letters up to 50g cost 3.80 francs and 5.50 francs respectively.

Telephone
The traditional coin-operated telephone is becoming extinct in France

and most have now been replaced by card-operated phones. Telephone cards (*télécarte*) are available in post offices or tobacconists. International calls are straightforward. To dial other countries first dial the international access code 19, wait for the second bleep, then the country code: Australia (61); Canada (1); Germany (49); Italy (39); Japan (81); the Netherlands (31); Spain (34); United Kingdom (44); United States (1). If you're using a US phone card, dial the company's access number: Sprint, Tel: 19 0087; AT&T, Tel: 19 0011; MCI, Tel: 19 0019.

Newspapers

Alsace has two daily newspapers: DNA (*Derniéres Nouvelles d'Alsace*) and *l'Alsace*. Both have a German edition. *L'Alsace* is distributed primarily in southern Alsace; the DNA in the north.

If you want to brush up your French with some current information you should stop by a kiosk and pick up the *Journal de l'Enfant* – a childrens' magazine published in Mulhouse. It reports on events in the Alsace region and in the world at large in clear, easily understood French.

SPORT

Hiking

The *Club Vosgien* (4 Rue de la Douane, F67000 Strasbourg) has marked out numerous hiking paths, and is also responsible for their maintenance. Details of hiker's cottages, providing basic overnight accommodation, are available from the Club. In addition, hiking maps for the various regions are available either directly from the club or from bookstores. Additional lodging is provided by Fermes-Auberges, the *Amis de la Nature* and the *Vosges Trotters*. You can obtain information about these at the *Comité Regional des Vosges*, 56 Avenue Aristide Briand, F68200 Mulhouse (89 43 25 50).

Canoeing

White-water canoeing in the Vosges mountains and gentler water travel in the Rhine river-plain: Alsace can offer both forms of sport. Information on watersports and rental facilities is provided by the *Comité Départmental de Canoe Kayak du Bas-Rhin*, 15 Rue de Généve, F67000 Strasbourg (88 35 27 20) or the *Club Nautique du Rhin*, 13 Rue Principale, F68000 Houssen (89 23 59 02). A guide to Alsatian watercourses can be obtained from the *Lique d'Alsace de Canoe Kayak*, 15 Rue de Généve, F67000 Strasbourg.

Golf

There are 18-hole golf courses in Il-lkirch-Graffernstaden near Strasbourg (88 61 72 29) and in Chalampé near Mulhouse Golfe de l'Ile du Rhin (89 26 07 86).

Horse Riding

Information about the many opportunities for horse-riding holidays in Alsace is provided by the *Association Alsacienne de Tourisme Equestre*, 78 Rue de l'Oberhardt, F68000 Colmar (89 79 38 48).

Fishing

Fishing licenses can be obtained from local tourist offices or city halls; information is available from the *Fédération Départementale des Associations de Pêche et de Pisciculture*, 1 Rue de Nomény, Strasbourg.

Hang-gliding

Information about schools and equipment rental is provided by the *Comité Départmentale de Vol Libre*, 35 Rue Jean-Martin, F68200 Mulhouse (89 59 18 39) or the *Lique de Leste de Vol Libre*, 4 Rue Strauss Durkheim, F67000 Strasbourg (88 36 49 38.

Winter Sport

Cross-country paths and ski-lifts beckon enthusiasts to the High Vosges, where there is usually sufficient snow cover. To find out where you can ski, inquire at the *Office de Tourisme* at F68370 Orbey (89 58 80 50).

Skiing courses are offered at almost all winter sport centres in the Vosges, among them the *Ferme-Auberge Steinlebach*, F68610 Le Markstein (89 82 61 87) or the *Centre les Genets d'Or*, 129 La Chapelle, F68650 Le Bonhomme (89 47 51 27). Information on ski lifts and schools is also available from the *Centre École de Ski de Fond*, F67000 Strasbourg (89 97 33 57).

Creative Holidays

Courses in weaving, silk-painting, pottery-making and wood-painting are all available in Alsace. Information can be obtained through tourist offices. The *Rélais Départmental du Tourisme Rural*, 103 Rue de Hausbergen, F67300 Schiltigheim (88 62 45 09) and the *Centre les Genets d'Or*, 129 La Chapelle, F68650 le Bonhomme (89 47 51 27) specialise in this area.

Holidays for the Handicapped

Information on events, holidays and accommodation for the handicapped (*Loisir-vacances des Handicaps*) is available through the *Chambre de Commerce et d'Industrie*, 1 Place de la Gare, F68000 Colmar (89 23 99 40). The *Association de Paralysés* offers a hotel guide for the handicapped – 22 Rue du Père Guérin, F75013 Paris.

Cooking Courses

A good source of information on all culinary questions is the *Centre d'Information du Vin d'Alsace*, BP145, F68000 Colmar. Also, the *Relais Départmental du Tourisme Rural, Maison de L'Agriculture*, 103 Route de Hausbergen, F67300 Schiltigheim (88 62 45 09 can further help those fans of

Alsatian cuisine who wish to learn the secrets of its original recipes directly from experts. Both organisations can also provide information about wine seminars.

Environmental Protection

The Alsatians are the champions as far as associations go: nowhere else in France are there as many leagues and alliances and this also applies in the area of environmental concerns. The AFRPN (*Association Fédérative Régional pour la Protection de la Nature*) regularly organises weekend tours with an emphasis on nature conservation. Information: 17 Rue Général Zimmer, F67000 Strasbourg (88 37 07 58).

ART & Photo CREDITS

Photography	**Hans-Jurgen Truöl** *and*
54	**Alice Bommer**
6/7, 10/11	**Bildagentur Anne Haman**
11, 53, 105, 106, 107, 116	**Editions La Cicogne**
16, 17, 24, 61, 86, 87,	**Joachim Ott**
88, 89, 90, 91, 92, 93, 94, 95,	
96, 99, 100, 101, 110, 119	
Cover Design	**Klaus Geisler**
Cartography	**Berndtson & Berndtson**

INSIGHT GUIDES

COLORSET NUMBERS

You'll find the colorset number on the spine of each Insight Guide.

INSIGHT *Pocket* GUIDES

EXISTING & FORTHCOMING TITLES:

Aegean Islands	Ireland	Phuket
Algarve	Istanbul	Prague
Alsace	Jakarta	Provence
Athens	**K**athmandu	**R**hodes
Bali	*Bikes & Hikes*	Rome
Bali Bird Walks	Kenya	**S**abah
Bangkok	Kuala Lumpur	San Francisco
Barcelona	**L**isbon	Sardinia
Bavaria	Loire Valley	Scotland
Berlin	London	Seville/Grenada
Bhutan	**M**acau	Seychelles
Boston	Madrid	Sikkim
Brittany	Malacca	Singapore
Brussels	Mallorca	South California
Budapest &	Malta	Southeast England
Surroundings	Marbella/	Sri Lanka
Canton	*Costa del Sol*	St Petersburg
Chiang Mai	Miami	Sydney
Costa Blanca	Milan	**T**enerife
Costa Brava	Morocco	Thailand
Cote d'Azur	Moscow	Tibet
Crete	Munich	Turkish Coast
Denmark	**N**epal	Tuscany
Florence	New Delhi	**V**enice
Florida	New York City	Vienna
Gran Canaria	North California	**Y**ogyakarta
Hawaii	**O**slo/Bergen	Yugoslavia's
Hong Kong	**P**aris	*Adriatic Coast*
Ibiza	Penang	

• •

United States: **Houghton Mifflin Company, Boston MA 02108**
Tel: (800) 2253362 Fax: (800) 4589501

Canada: **Thomas Allen & Son, 390 Steelcase Road East**
Markham, Ontario L3R 1G2
Tel: (416) 4759126 Fax: (416) 4756747

Great Britain: **GeoCenter UK, Hampshire RG22 4BJ**
Tel: (256) 817987 Fax: (256) 817988

Worldwide: **Höfer Communications Singapore 2262**
Tel: (65) 8612755 Fax: (65) 8616438

“ I was first drawn to the Insight Guides by the excellent "Nepal" volume. I can think of no book which so effectively captures the essence of a country. Out of these pages leaped the Nepal I know – the captivating charm of a people and their culture. I've since discovered and enjoyed the entire Insight Guide Series. Each volume deals with a country or city in the same sensitive depth, which is nowhere more evident than in the superb photography. ”

Sir Edmund Hillary